WOMEN LEGISLATORS IN INDIAN POLITICS

About the Author

Pitam Singh, (*b.* 1955) is an engineer turned into social scientist basically. He is a senior officer in the Planning Commission, Government of India and has been working in the Industry Division since 1991. He has his first degree in Chemical Engineering and holds diploma in Computer Aided Design. He has done his Master's degree (M.Sc.) in Development Studies from University of Bath U.K. and Ph.D. in Sociology from CCS University, Meerut. He is a guest faculty to GGSIP University, Delhi and has guided many students in their M.Sc. dessertation. He is an Associate Member of Indian Institute of Chemical Engineers Jadavpur, Kolkata. This book is a part of his Ph.D. thesis and the various assignments undertaken at University of Bath and University of Reading, U.K. He has also served M/s National Fertilizers Limited, Panipat and Cochin Refineries Limited, Cochin as Engineer and Deputy Manager of more than a decade.

WOMEN LEGISLATORS
IN
INDIAN POLITICS

by
PITAM SINGH

CONCEPT PUBLISHING COMPANY, NEW DELHI-110059

ISBN : 81-8069-019-9

First Published 2003

Published and Printed by
Ashok Kumar Mittal
Concept Publishing Company
A/15-16, Commercial Block, Mohan Garden,
New Delhi-110059

Phones : 25351460, 25351794
Fax : 091-11-25357103
Email : publishing@conceptpub.com

SOMPAL
MEMBER
PLANNING COMMISION
GOVERNMENT OF INDIA

YOJANA BHAWAN
PARLIAMENT STREET
NEW DELHI-110001
PHONE : 3096569
FAX : 3096568
e-mail:sompal@yojana.nic.in

सत्यमेव जयते

FOREWORD

India is the largest democracy of the world. It is governed by a written Constitution containing immaculate details of various components of a federal polity assigning specific roles-duties and rights-to the citizens and the various governing entities right from the Central Government to the State Governments, to the administration at district, block, taluka and the municipal committee/village levels. Fortunately, all these arrangements and the three wings of our democracy, i.e., the legislature, the executive and the judiciary have been functioning smoothly. The fourth estate, the Press has been almost as free as in any other democratic country. Independence of judiciary and human rights have reasonably been upheld. However, there have been some pitfalls. One of these is the lack of participation and representation of certain sections of society, especially women. The recent 73rd and 74th Amendments to the Constitution though have been major steps forward in fulfilling this gap. Elections to all urban local bodies, panchayats at block and district level have been held giving 33 per cent reservation to women, which have been functioning since last three years. India is the only country, which has gone ahead with such radical affirmative action in women empowerment.

An analysis of the democratic system and representation of various sections of population in our country reveals that the participation of women in the political process has been far below their counterpart. The reasons for this are well known, which include tradition, physiology, psychology, lack of encouragement and pre-occupation with domestic affairs. There may be many more reasons, which hinder women's active involvement in political and administrative decision making. The declining sex ratio, increasing violence and crime against women and their marginalized status in employment, education and health sectors make the position quite obvious. As there has been no major study at national level on this vital issue, it is imperative to examine the possibility of enhanced role of women in modern Indian society.

The book presents the findings of a study of women legislators in Uttar Pradesh (UP) Assembly. Interestingly, UP is politically a very sensitive state and has always been in the forefront of the national scene. It continues to play and important role in deciding the leadership at the Centre. The State provides specific situation by virtue of its large size, density of population, largest electorates, largest assembly, complex social composition, socio-cultural history and being a hub of political activities.

The book attempts to analyse the role of women legislators and their involvement in two different but related arenas of political process; namely, the legislatures and party organizations. It covers mainly five areas : socio-economic profiles of women legislators, the route they have taken to reach their positions, their performance, the kind of issues raised in the assembly and the problems they faced. The book examines all the women legislators elected in all the elections right from the first in 1952 to the last in 2002 and thus is a longitudinal study of 50 years of political participation of women legislators.

The analysis is likely to provide valuable input to policy makers and help fine-tune the policies on women reservation, which has been a key issue, debated for a long time. The book will be a precious addition to all libraries and extremely useful reference for researchers and workers interested in the field of women empowerment.

SOMPAL

PREFACE

This book presents the study of women legislators of Uttar Pradesh focusing on five main areas; the social profile of women legislators; the routes they have taken to get to their political position, their role performance, the policy areas in which they were involved, the issues they raise in the Assembly and their social and cultural barriers to participate in politics. The book is a longitudinal study of 50 years of women legislators covering first election in 1952 to the last (fourteenth) election in 2002. This is merely a qualitative exercise that is geared towards generating a debate on the issue of women political participation in India and tends to raise a number of questions rather than provide answers.

The work that ultimately become this project begin in 1996 as an academic exercise, when I got registered as a research scholar at Chaudhary Charan Singh University, Meerut, was completed in the year 2001. In this period, three important, events took place in U.P. related to study, which changed the data on States population, geographical area, political position as well as many other socio-economic indicators without having impact on the findings. First event, U.P. was divided in two parts creating "Uttaranchal" carving out from it and bifurcating the hill regions, comprising 13 districts covering an area of 53483 square kilometers and population of 84,79,562. The second, State Government issued a new notification for caste classification and some castes, which were in general category earlier were brought under a new class, the Other Backward Caste (OBC) resulting in changes in reservation policy for legislators in the assembly. And the third, fourteenth assembly elections were declared and conducted in 2002 first time after bifurcation of the State and it was thought fit to cover the last elections to make the work quite recent. Surprisingly, all these developments have no significant effects on the findings except on the parameter's profile of State.

The some of the problems, faced during the present study is worth mentioning. Keeping track of poll related general and specific information and the data had been an arduous task. The list of women legislators given in Election Commission's Reports seldom matched with the list available in the who's who published by the State's Vidhan Sabha Secretariat. It is because, Election Commission provides the list of those who were declared elected in a particular elections, while, one can soon resign after the elections but Vidhan Sabha keeps the records only of the sitting legislators. The other thing, a women can contest elections from more than one constituencies and may be declared elected from all and therefore, her name will appear in the Election Commission's Report at more than one places, whereas in Vidhan Sabha records it would be seen only at one place.

The majority of women legislators expressed their inabilities to send a written response to our questionnaire, collecting information on specific issues became extremely tardy. This further worsened by the paucity of literature, especially on women legislators.

Another set of difficulty was arranging the timings for meeting with women legislators for their interviews, which proved to be an extremely challenging and arduous task in terms of their availability and also willingness to cooperate. Persistent and continuous efforts, therefore, had to be made to contact them. One of the major constraints of the present study has been the limited availability of the women legislators.

The weeklies and fortnightlies had commissioned specialists to give the best information. All this information has been carefully called, re-edited and re-arranged in a presentable form in the book. Party documents and Election Commission's press release and reports have been best use of. Presentation of Election data has been a challenging job. The listed data and information has been carefully collated. It is based on Election Commission's documents (Reports from 1952-2002).

The present book does not claim to be complete in itself, it has a beginning but no end. This leaves the scope for further study and debate on the issue of women representation in the political bodies.

The book (I hope) will answer many questions developmental planners will have about the aspects of women reservation in the highest political and decision making bodies and other more technical questions that political and social scientists regard as salient.

New Dehli
1st November, 2002

PITAM SINGH

ACKNOWLEDGEMENTS

Any project work is an exhaustive task and cannot be completed single handedly. Straightway, I want to place my sincere thanks to the staff of University of Bath, UK especially Dr. Geoff Wood, the then Director, Development Studies, who recognized my abilities to analyse various developmental issues from inter-disciplinary angle knowing fully well that I was an engineer and ill-educated about the socio-economic problems of the developing countries and more generally the problems of gender empowerment in India. He always kept encouraging me writing about the socio-political problems during my Master's Degree (M.Sc.) in Development Studies at Universities of Bath, UK. His guidance as lecture on the subject gave me insight dynamics of social science.

The present book is improved version of my Ph.D. thesis. The role of research supervisor is very important as his help starts from the day of the "idea" of project conceived and continues through out the life of the project, till it comes to the final stage. He provides ideology, design and methodology to the research work and dedicates his valuable and considerable time. My heartfelt gratitude to Dr. J.K. Pundir, Professor and Head, Department of Sociology, CCS University, Meerut, my guide who has not only provided guidance to me in this work but also in my personal endeavor. I am also grateful to his wife Smt. Servesh for her hospitality during my visits to their home.

I am grateful to Shri Sompal, Member, Planning Commission who has not only spared and relieved me from office work to complete the book but also provided valuable suggestions. My special thanks to Dr. Ved Parkash, former Adviser (Education) Planning Commission, Delhi and now Secretary, UGC, who took pains to go through the manuscript and suggested valuable changes. I am also thankful to Shri Prem Singh, my colleague, a SRO in Planning Commission who has always inspired me and pressed me hard to complete the book. The staff members of Planning Commission Library and UP Vidhan Sabha Secretariat and Library are praiseworthy and I am thankful to them also.

I am also thankful to the respondents who have not only spared their valuable time to sit for an interview but eagerly come forward to express their views about the specific issues, whenever asked for.

Finally, my special thanks to my wife Smt. Kamlesh and to my children whom time I encroached upon to write this book. They always encouraged me to go ahead and completed the book whenever I felt exhausted.

PITAM SINGH

Contents

1

INTRODUCTION

The Research Design

1.1 Background and Rationale of the Problem

The last two decades have been marked by critical activity both of women and by women. The growing body of literature and evidence on women's integral involvement in varied structures and processes of society have brought gender to the centrestage of all the developmental efforts. "It is now widely recognized that seemingly well worked out plans and programmes being both gender-biased and gender blind can have disastrous consequences for women" (Kumari, 1994: 33). Efforts are, therefore, being made to develop alternate strategies and discourses that are both gender-sensitive and gender-just. Such attempts are, however, yet to be satisfactorily incorporated into the political processes and decision-making bodies. Although the post-independence era in India has witnessed overall development and progress in varied arena and sectors, women's involvement and role in public life has not made much headway. "The number, extent, nature and levels of women participating in politics and playing politically active roles are far from being satisfactory" (ibid: 33).

"Politics is one field where the evidence of increasing participation by women is still not very impressive in most of the countries" (Atal, 1993:17). "*While substantial gains have been made by the women's movement over the decades in India, this has not been adequately reflected in the representation of women in position of power*" (Kumari, 1996: 1). Today it is widely recognized that a precondition for any developmental effort, which is environmentally harmonious and that safeguards human rights, is the participation and involvement of women in this process. In fact, "the crux of the present world order is the issue of ecology, development and gender, and therefore, needs specific attention" (Mohanty, 2000: 1). Gender inequalities are pervasive in various layers of social existence as its tentacles are spread across various segments of society. Women, who constitute approximately half of the population, have been subjected to the tyranny and oppression of a patriarchal order for centuries and in fact most of them, both in elite and non-elite societies, are suffering from in one form or the other even today. Although, several provisions for empowering them have been made in the Constitution of our country, they are not given equal status that they legitimately deserve in the society. It is this aspect that needs to be closely examined with a view to identifying the desired reforms to shape up the future of our posterity. It is, therefore, extremely essential to identify and understand the ground realities to eradicate the menace of gender inequality from the society.

Women are poorly represented in the rank of power, policy and decision-making. "Women make up less than five per cent of the world's heads of the State, heads of major corporations and top positions in international organizations" (Mohanty, 2000: 1). Women are not just behind in politics and managerial equity, they are a long way behind in other spheres of life as well. This is in spite of the fact that women are found in large numbers in low-level political parties, trade unions and business. This situation prevails all over the globe. "In Britain, where women were granted franchise way back in 1918, the first woman member took her seat in 1919. In 1970 election, only 26 were returned to the House of Commons, which constituted only 4.1 per cent of the total membership. In US, where women got franchise as far back as August 1920, there were only 10 members, 2.03 per cent only, in House of Representatives, which was comprised 435 members in the early 1970s" (Kumari, 1996: 5).

In India, there is a great hiatus between constitutional guarantees and the active representation of women. The right to constitutional equalities was supplemented by legal equality by the passage of a number of Acts through which traditional inequalities in respect of marriage, divorce and property rights were eliminated. Notwithstanding of these Constitutional and legal provisions, women representation is almost negligible even at the lowest rung of political hierarchy. This is the scenario of all the political parties regardless of their size and function. Lest we talk about their representation in the Parliament and the Legislative Assemblies, the better it is. "In fact, the highest representation that women have ever enjoyed was 9.0 per cent in Parliament in 1999 election (Rana, 2000: 74), 9.11 per cent in State Assemblies and about 12.96 per cent in the Council of Ministers" (Kumari, 1996: 2). It is well known that while women constitute about 50 per cent of the total electorate, they have never been able to get adequate representation in any Lok Sabha as well as in the State Assemblies and what is worse is that their representation has an incremental decline.

"Many women today are coming forward to join the decision-making process by joining the Indian Administrative Services, the Indian Police Service, judiciary, political parties, local self-government bodies. But at each and every step, they face '*Laxman Rekha*'. In spite of their readiness to take up challenges, they get limited political opportunity" (Patel, 1996: 28). Women politicians have to face a lot of harassment from vested interests. With the criminalisation of politics, women not only face character assassination and threats, but at times they also become soft target of violence. In fact, in the past, there have been a number of incidents of physical assaults, rape and murder of such women folks. "In Bengal, a female officer of the UNICEF was brutally raped and murdered. A woman activist in Maharashtra was kidnapped, confined and repeatedly raped by the activist of a political party. Similar cases have been reported in Andhra Pradesh, Goa, Punjab and Assam" (Patel, 1996: 32).

With the increasing demand to bring women forward into the political processes and decision-making bodies, their involvement at the grassroots level acquires special significance, not merely in terms of political training but also to ensure that those who are at the helm of affairs are the true representatives of people's interests. "Mere increase in the number of women officials will not ensure empowerment of women but the goals and attitude of these women politicians towards women specific dimensions must be in the women's interest" (Patel, 1996: 26). The existing discrepancy of women's majority status as voters (and also participants in other political processes) and minority status as decision-makers, and to ensure and enhance the involvement and participation of women in decision-making bodies calls for immediate attention for analysis of women's participation and activities at grassroots level and state level politics as well.

In such situation, a critical analysis of both "Gender in Politics" and "Politics of Gender" is essential to seek answers to some of the questions raised in the present study. The historical under-representation of women in decision-making bodies is inextricably linked with the low and inferior status of women in the society and, therefore, calls for an analysis of different relationships and the constant conjunction of varied forces and elements: economic, social, cultural as also political which hinder women's meaningful participation in political processes and decision-making bodies. Therefore, the purpose of the present investigation is to study the socio-economic background of the women legislators of the state of Uttar Pradesh and their involvement in politics.

The earlier studies attempted so far on the participation of women in politics are mainly confined to their voting behaviour or at the best partaking of position as candidates, member of legislatures and ministers. The present study, however, focuses on the participation of women as legislators in UP Assembly. It is believed that such participation will be the springboard for positions, which are vital in contributing to the decision-making in the public sphere, as women can then reach such positions gracefully and easily, without having to struggle.

The question of women's participation in political process and decision-making bodies forms a key concern of the women's movement in India. An analysis of the democratic system and representation of various sections of the population therein reveals that women are far behind than their male counterparts. Their under-representation becomes critical especially in the context of declining sex ratio, increasing violence and crimes against women and their marginalized status in employment, education and health sectors.

Meanwhile, there are certain basic questions which women's movement has to ask of itself and caution itself against. This will relate to the definition of the concept of political participation itself. Will the participation of women on a vast scale in voting change the nature of democratic functioning from that of patriarchal model to one of gender based egalitarianism? If the power of voting has to make the citizens the sovereigns, the majority of the poor and rural voters would be the sovereigns of India, and the State would have emerged as that of the poor, but the fact until now remains that it is just the reverse. If holding positions is the indication or the means of women's development, then there should be correlation between the extent of development in the region and electoral results. In reality, Kerala, the most developed state from the point of view of women's development, holds also highest percentage of women voting. But it has a very low percentage of women contesting the elections to enter into the law making bodies.

Equally pertinent is the question as to whether the women who have had made to the legislative and executive positions have been able and exerted themselves to promote the interest of women. It is one thing for them to hold political positions and power but the other thing for them is to use such positions for the empowerment of their own tribe. "Women legislators are not taken seriously or given responsible tasks like introducing motions" (Kaushik, 1996: 40). This may not be totally correct and there also may be a trend for the better in recent times. But the general picture is still true that the women executives and legislators have to put up a difficult and sustained struggle in order to bring about the steps needed to sensitize colleagues and others and to promote women's interests. This aspect, therefore, needs to be further studied. It is hence necessary to undertake studies to find out whose benefits women participation in politics is directed for? What impact has this participation made on the policies and the system over a period?

For effecting this impact, it is equally necessary to assess the level at which this participation is taking place. Mere numbers are not enough; it has to be situated at levels, which are significant and effective. "Impressive participation in the political process, formal and informal, is not goals in themselves, they are means and strategy for achieving something more fundamental, which the group can do, only when its participation touches upon the structure of politics itself' (Kaushik, 1996: 40). Therefore, one has to identify the broader process of the political structure and the way power is arranged in a particular society. The ideology of state, the interrelationship between the important components in its structure like class, caste and gender, and its basic developmental goals are essential in understanding the repercussions of participation. Often a vastly expanded participation and wide mobilization of a socially weak community, in this context women, has led to the strengthening of the present pattern of development rather than directing this pattern to their own development. Even values like equality (constitutional, political, economic) or right (property, access to resources) may be meaningful only when women possess and exercise them for bringing about a change in their own position as well as of the society; otherwise they will merely add up to strengthening reinforcing the existing social system by operating within the framework of patriarchy. Values like equality and rights, concept like participation and mobilization need to be constantly kept before them the objectives of the client group.

Any assessment of political participation of women in a state like Uttar Pradesh has to start by asking the questions like whether such participation has led bringing about or moving towards improvement in the lives of women or whether it simply makes life more livable for women. Whether such participation by women either as individuals or as a group has meant working out alternate strategies for development as well as structure of power. Whether the political intentions which women seek to make start with women as points of departure or merely help them infiltrate systematically in the existing hierarchies of power, thereby lending themselves to becoming women performers or even worse. If increasing participation has to have any meaning for women, such participation should be based on the widespread and well-orchestrated mobilization of women on the central issue of women's oppression and subordinate status in society and family. The outcome of such a study may suggest that where the assembly and the political parties may reach with such interventions as reservations for women in decision making bodies, especially at the state levels.

The analysis of political participation of women in UP would have to be combined with few components like (a) the extent, level and nature of women's participation in the political process of state, by way of both formal and non-formal institutions, (b) the impact and significance of such participation for women's rights and living conditions, and (c) the type of feminist issues that were raised in the course of this participation.

Keeping in view the above three criteria, one can assess the nature and extent of women's participation in some of the significant formal and informal process of any state politics. The freedom struggle, peasant and trade union movements, the electoral and legislative institutions, the local government (Panchayati Raj systems), the administrative and judicial functioning are some of the formal processes wherein the participation of women can be evaluated. There are also institutions like political parties, interest and lobby groups, religious and caste movements, where the women are participating increasingly. The present study has focused only on the women legislators of UP Assembly to assess their position because it was not possible to cover all the above areas in one volume.

There have been some studies to understand the role of women in Indian politics. Ranjana Kumari (1996) in her study on women has found that the social and cultural barriers have stood in the way of women coming out of the traditional way of life to participate in the political process. Shanta Bhatt (1995) in her study has examined the constraints of Indian women politicians. Pravin N. Seth (1979) has studied social background of women members of Parliament and has found that most of the women MPs belong to well off and highly educated families.

Parvathamma and Jongem (1969) have studied 53 scheduled caste members of Parliament (MPs) to study their educational background, including caste and subcaste difference among them. Satish Sabberwal (1971) has studied social mobility and change among some scheduled castes at individual as well as at group level from closed status group caste to open status group. He finds that, in recent times, economic and political systems have increased their autonomy in relation to the caste structure.

Many studies show that the women politicians face peculiar

problems in their political life, which are totally unknown to their male counterparts. These inhibit their performance in the legislative assembly. "The reasons for women's diminished role in political arena include traditions, physiology, lack of vertical mobility, concern for home and family, psychology and lack of patronage, particularly from senior women politicians" (Bhatt, 1995: 90). There may be many more reasons, which hinder women's active involvement in politics. In fact, studies on such issues have been very rare and no systematic and comprehensive study appears to have been done on this issue.

It is, indeed, this reason that necessitates an analysis of issues that are responsible for limiting women's participation in the political process. Thus, the present study has made an attempt to analyse the background, role and involvement of women in politics and the constraints thereof, if any. The study has been undertaken to focus only on the women legislators in Uttar Pradesh Assembly.

1.2 The Statement of Problem : Research Questions

To illustrate the main arguments, the present study focuses upon the following five specific questions :

(i) Who are the women leaders in UP?
(ii) How have they emerged as leaders?
(iii) What role do they play?
(iv) What kind of issues do they raise in the Assembly? and
(v) Whether their social and cultural barriers have stood in their way to participate in politics?

The first question "who are the women leaders in UP" implies that what is the socio-economic, educational and other background of women leaders in this state. *Leaders, in the present study mean the elected women legislators to UP Assembly.* There are many other leaders identifiable through positional approach like Members of Parliament (MPs), Members of Legislative Council, Members of Municipal Committees, Members of Block Samities, Members of Village Panchayats, Sarpanchs, etc. The present study is limited to understand the background of the women legislators—their caste, marital status, age, family profile, occupation and their education.

The second question takes note of the process through which they have emerged as leaders. This indicates the contributing factors and the processes through which women legislators have achieved their position of leadership. The process means whether through election, selection and nomination. Contributing factors include previous participation in socio-political activities, socialization, chance factors, situation which forces them to get involved in some struggle, or any other political training and participation. All these factors have been studied with reference to those women legislators who are identified as respondents.

The third question is "what role do they play?" This question means their performance in public life. As leaders, they are expected to play some roles, which are different from the roles of common women. By virtue of occupying a position, i.e. status of a leader at certain level what has been their contribution in the upliftment and empowerment of the women in particular and society in general. This also involves their role for the welfare and upliftment of their community people, for the youths and indirectly their role for strengthening the position and support of other male leaders.

This question has been searching answer for the roles of women legislators in their party organizations and forums, the share of responsibilities and leadership roles women have taken during elections, etc.

The fourth question is related to their performance in the legislative assembly. This is to examine the range and depth of women's participation and their involvement in the assembly proceedings, particularly in raising issues, moving resolutions, proposing motions, etc. This question has also involved an analysis of 'women' as a group in the assembly, the occasions and issues on which they may cut across party lines and join hands together.

The fifth question is to examine the hindrance mainly due to social and cultural barriers that the women legislators face while entering into active politics and performing their role as leader. Besides, some of the major issues, which either facilitate or limit women's participation in the political process, have also been examined in this question.

1.3 Area of Study

The study has been undertaken in the state of Uttar Pradesh. Uttar Pradesh (UP) is politically a very sensitive and an important state in a number of ways. UP which is socially more backward than a number of other states have sent more women into the Central and State Legislatures. It has the largest legislative assembly, sends largest number of MPs in the Parliament and thus, it has always played a significant role in national politics by dominating on the national scene. UP sends as many as 80 MPs in the Lok Sabha and has 404 seats in the State Legislative assembly. The important leaders have always focused attention on this state. The state of UP has produced many men and women leaders of national and international repute. In fact, the first woman Prime Minister of India belonged to UP. Out of thirteen Prime Ministers of India elected so far, eight Prime Ministers were from Uttar Pradesh. More women members of the UP had become members in the Central Cabinet than women from any other state. Both formal and informal leadership can be observed in this state. That is why, UP has been selected for the present study. UP has the highest population in the country. In fact, there are only six countries in the world whose population is more than that of UP. This state provides a specific situation by its location, general reputation, social composition, having large women voters, socio-cultural history and important centre of political activities. The demographic and other important salient features of UP, position of women in state, their political activities and organisations and political parties they belong to have been dealt in one of the subsequent chapters.

1.4 Universe, Sample, Identification and Selection of Respondents

The UP Legislature consists of the Governor and the two houses known as the Legislative Council and the Legislative Assembly. At present, the Council has 100 members whilst the Assembly has 404 members excluding one member of Anglo-Indian community. The prime unit of the analysis has been women legislators in UP

Assembly. The women leaders, in the context of the study consist of all women legislators elected till fourteenth assembly elections held in UP so far and, therefore, constitutes the universe of the present study. A profile of all women legislators including all former women legislators of UP assembly was prepared and it was observed that about fifty-six women were elected as legislators more than once. Many of them represented continuously their constituencies as many times as seven. The study has also tried to find out the attitude of their male colleagues towards them to a limited extent.

The first Assembly Elections in UP were held in 1952 wherein eleven women legislators were Elected to the Assembly. The latest Assembly Elections in UP were held in 2002 and 26 women were elected. Mayawati contested elections from two constituencies and was declared elected from both, thus actual number of women elected in 2002 elections are 25. Since 1952, 14 assembly elections have been conducted in UP and a total of 255 women were elected in all. Out of 255 women legislators, 56 were elected more than once. A list was prepared of all and it was observed that 56 women have been repeatedly appearing at 166 places in the list. If 56 are excluded from 166 and the remainder 110 from 255, the total numbers of women legislators were reduced to 145. Out of these 145 legislators, 7 legislators have expired and 12 could not reply queries properly due to their poor health conditions coupled with old age, etc. Fifteen have not sent filled in questionnaires despite repeated reminders and persuasion. Sixteen have been elected first time in 2002 elections and also there is no information available about them regarding their age, education, family background, income, profession, etc. in the literature like *Who's Who* published by the UP Vidhan Sabha secretariat. There were also legislators who have expired, besides others who could not be contacted despite all efforts. Such cases have been deleted as the case of "sample mortality". Eventually, it left the total respondent as 95.

The election-wise number of women legislators and the year in which elections were held are given in Table 1.1. The name-wise, constituency-wise detailed list of women legislators and the respondents are placed at Appendix I. The research has primarily been analytical in content and nature. Of course, some comparison between some ex-women legislators and present women members in terms of their age, educational qualifications and legislative experience has been undertaken.

TABLE 1.1 : Number of Women Legislators in the UP Assembly

Sl. No.	*Year*	*Assembly*	*No. of Elected Women*	*Per cent*
1	1952	First	11	3.17
2	1957	Second	24	7.00
3	1962	Third	20	4.65
4	1967	Fourth	7	1.64
5	1969	Fifth	19	4.47
6	1974	Sixth	22	5.17
7	1977	Seventh	12	2.82
8	1980	Eighth	20	4.70
9	1985	Ninth	31	7.30
10	1989	Tenth	19	4.47
11	1991	Eleventh	10	2.35
12	1993	Twelfth	13	3.05
13	1996	Thirteenth	21	4.94
14	2002	Fourteenth	26	6.43
			Total = 255	Avg. 4.44

Source: *Who's Who*, published by Secretariat of UP Assembly and Election Commission's Reports (1952-2002).

There is some inconsistency in the figures given in the Report of the Election Commission and figures provided by the Assembly Secretariat. The difference in the figures may be because the Election Commission's reports contain the names of all the contestants who have been declared elected in a particular election. However, one may resigned soon after her/his election and same would not be appearing in the list provided by the Assembly Secretariat as it keeps records of sitting legislators only. Similarly, one candidate declared elected at more than one seat her name will appear at two or three places causing difference in figures. For example; In 2002 Elections, Mayawati had contested elections from two Constituencies (Harora and Bilsi) and was declared elected from both, thus Election Commission's Report contains her name as two candidates, which Vidhan Sabha secretariat as one. Similarly, in 1996 Elections, Mayawati had contested from two Constituencies and won from both. Later she resigned from both places after winning her elections as M.P. Omwati also resigned from her Nagina seat in 1976. Thus, Election Commission shows record of 21 women legislators while Vidhan Sadha 18 only.

1.5 Method of Data Collection

No single method appears to be useful to collect data on such a problem. Data were collected from primary and secondary sources and by (a) structured questionnaire and (b) interview schedule. Both the quantitative and qualitative methods have been used to seek information. The bulk of information was generated through the structured questionnaires. This was supplemented by the personal interviews in some cases. Relevant information for the present study was collected in three stages.

At the initial stage, a comprehensive and in-depth analysis of the existing literature on the political process and decision-making bodies in particular was made. Both the formal and informal available sources were explored to collect required information.

In the second stage, a structured questionnaire was formulated to extract information from women legislators on specific areas and issues. The questionnaire was designed to obtain information on :

i. Personal life,
ii. Involvement in politics,
iii. Association with political party/parties,
iv. Involvement in electoral politics,
v. Role and legislature politics and proceedings,
vi. Role as a minister/legislator,
vii. Response to certain general and women specific issues, and
viii. Suggestions on an increased and qualitatively better participation for/of women in political process and decision making bodies.

The questionnaires formulated were mailed to the women legislators. As only three women legislators sent back the first round of questionnaire (although majority of them confirmed having received questionnaires), another round of questionnaires were sent to them. After persistent reminders only 40 women legislators responded with filled in questionnaires.

In the third stage, simultaneous efforts had to be made to contact them in person for interviews. With the selected women legislators both sitting and former (40), personal interviews were held.

Few ex-women legislators are now Members of Parliament (MPs), who due to their extremely busy schedule spent only about 20-25 minutes; the rest had long conversations with the researcher, approximately of two hours. The selected group of men legislators too had concerns and responded to the questionnaire. Although, by and large, slower in their responses but willing to share information, views and experiences, they were not categorical on certain issues, especially those concerning their respective political parties. Therefore, beyond a point, in a conversation the gender element (i.e. specific reactions arising out of the respondent being a 'woman' or 'man') got disclosed and responses were merely those of a politician *per se*.

Seven cases of women legislators have been described in detail as the case studies. These were selected taking into account the representation of different castes among the women legislators and different leadership positions held by them. One of the important criteria for selection of the case studies was their experience as legislators, the number of times they had represented their constituencies and their position as minister. Legislators belonging to the scheduled castes and OBCs and the legislators from the different parts of the state have been considered while taking up the case studies. While describing the case studies, interviews of the legislators, observations, supplementary information through knowledgeable persons and available in their life history in various records have been used. With the co-operation of the legislators as also our own perceptions and preparations, it could be possible to collect required information for this study.

1.6 Analysis of the Data

The information furnished by the respondents and collected from various other sources was transferred from the notes, diaries and the interview schedules questionnaires on to the data sheets prior to its analysis. The huge data on various aspects have been analyzed and arranged in tables for interpretation. The data were subjected to chi-square and correlation analysis. Case materials, however, were qualitatively analyzed. On the background variables a quantitative method has been used as a device of analysis. The relationship of various factors has been indicated on the basis of numerical distribution presented in the tables. Thus, the data of 95 respondents have been analyzed qualitatively and also to some extent quantitatively.

1.7 Concepts/Terms

There are some concepts, which have been frequently used for understanding of the empirical materials on the women legislators. The following concepts as technical terms and tools for precision and abstraction have repeatedly been used:

1.7.1 *Politics and Political Participation*

"Politics refers to the functioning of a whole array of public institutions and forces which are involved in moulding the lives of people by way of decisions and policies that impinge upon their relations with one another" (Kaushik, 1996: 35). 'Politics' is often defined in a very narrow term as the electoral participation in democracy. The varied activities that are performed by a person in an elected position or as part of the voter's duty, defined as political participation. This is because such participation is expected to be the springboard of decision making in the public sphere that, in turn, is denoted as power.

"The concept of politics has, by and large, been defined either in terms of "process" or in terms of the "peace" or "place" where it happens, i.e. in terms of the 'arena' or the institutional forms (i.e. parliament, assemblies, etc.)" (Kumari, 1994: 34). However, there does exist an overlapping between the two. Thus, for instance, those who subscribe to the 'arena' concept may regard it as a process but confine this process of politics to certain kinds of institutions and organizations. Broadly defining, politics refers to a whole gamut of structures and forces that affect people's lives by way of decisions and policies. It involves not merely the availability of opportunities, rights, liberties and justice to both individuals and the groups, but also the extent to which they are availed of and exercised.

1.7.2 *Leader*

'Leader' literally means a person who leads or has the capacity to lead. He/she can understand the complexities of the social structures, which are the base of politics, education, economy and social status. Leader has been understood in two different senses: (a) "to excel, to be in advance, to be prominent", and (b) " to guide others, to be head of organization, to hold command". In the first sense, the leadership is identified with individual pre-eminence and in the later sense, it is identified with organizational talent. The leader exercises the power of a society, of a group, the government or an institution for a common cause. The power also indicates authority. The leader is one who has power and authority (Majumdar, 1967: 278). In any group, these powers have to be activated for the accomplishment of certain ends. The leadership act represents a choice of these instruments of power. The leader cannot and will not always rely on these instruments of power. "He should effect the behaviour of the followers in a situation" (Terry, 1972). He has to energize and influence the people, in a common effort, to achieve the purpose of an enterprise.

Leader, operationally, defined as one who occupies power position in any organization or association in the government or otherwise. *In the present study, the women legislators who have been occupying position in the most important decision-making body, namely, the State Legislature have been considered as leaders.*

It is an accepted phenomenon that the upbringing of the depressed or women depends largely upon the quality of organized leadership made available to the people. The characteristics have been tried with respect to the performance of the women leaders at national level involved in the process of social, political and economic changes, in general, and women legislators in the Assembly of Uttar Pradesh, in particular.

1.7.3 *Power*

"Power is defined as the capacity to influence the decisions of others — groups as well as the individuals. Power is derived from the economic, political, social status of an individual or a group" (Pore Kumud, 1993: 59). The politically powerful makes important policy decisions through popularly elected bodies at various levels. Power has been used here to denote the capacity to influence decisions, particularly in the assembly and other group forums.

1.7.4 *Elite*

Pareto suggests that "Let us assume that in every branch of human activities, each individual is given an index which stands as a sign of his capacity in very much the same way as grades are given in the various subjects in examinations in school. So let us make a class of the people who have the highest indices in their branch of activity and to that class give the name of elite." Mosca defines the elite "as an organized minority, obeying a simple impulse, which holds dominance over the un-organized majority".

For Laswell (1950) the elite are, "the holders of the high positions in a given society". Cooley refers to the elite as "group that emerges to the position of leadership and influence at every social level". Nodal has defined the elite as a "body of persons enjoying a position of pre-eminence over all others". According to Kom Houser, the term elite is used in respect of "those positions in a social structures which are super-ordinate such that the incumbent claims and are granted social superiority". The term is also used to refer to the functions attached to such positions, especially the special responsibility to form and define value standard in a certain social sphere. T.B. Bottomore has defined the term as "the elite is now generally applied in fact to functional, mainly occupational groups, which have high status (for whatever reason) in a society".

An analysis of the above-mentioned definitions brings out the fact that such elements as superiority, power and organizations are important in defining the term elite. Thus, we may think of the elite as those who are regarded as superior, influential and are held in high esteem by the people. They may or may not have formal positions in politics and the government but they are in a position to influence the decision-making process, set values and uphold them.

1.7.5 *Role*

First of all, it was systematically used by Linton and later, based on the meaning given by Linton, R.K. Merton had developed a theory of role in the context of social structure. Status means a position in a social system occupied by the designated individuals; by role, the behavioural enacting of the patterned expectations attributed to that position (Merton, 1968: 422). Thus, role in this sense incorporates behaviour patterns of the social position in accordance with the expectations by others from that position. These expectations are culturally defined and indicate relationship of the position holders and other participants in social structure. Thus, in the present context, the concept of role has been used to understand the behaviour pattern of the women leaders and women legislators in particular, that has followed from their positions as a legislator and is expected by others in the respective fields of their activities as leaders.

1.7.6 *Influential : The Local and the Cosmopolitan*

The persons to whom the other people turn up for help or advice regarding various types of personal decisions (e.g. choice of a job, educational plan, selection of books and furniture, etc.) are known as influentials. Of course, this influential exercises influence indirectly through major political matters and other administrative decisions, which affect large number of people (Merton, 1968: 443-445).

There are two types of influentials, the local and the cosmopolitan. Both differ in orientation. Local is largely confined to his local community and this is essentially his world. He devotes little thought or energy to the larger society. He is preoccupied with local problems to the virtual exclusion of national and international scene. He is strictly parochial. Contrary to this is the cosmopolitan type. He has some interest in the local community and maintains a minimum of relations within the community since he too exerts influence there. He is also oriented significantly to the world outside the local community and regards himself as an integral part of that world. He resides in the local community but lives in the larger society. Thus, the local type is parochial, the cosmopolitan is accumical.

The concept of local and cosmopolitan influential, thus formulated by Merton, would be used in examining and classifying the women leaders whether they have local cosmopolitan in orientation as described above. As used by Merton, participation in a number of organizations at various levels and getting leadership positions by them such as the Chief Minister of the state and Ministers at the Centre is an indicator of cosmopolitan type.

1.7.7 *Reference Groups (Models)*

Merton (1968) states, "That man acts in a social frame of reference fielded by groups of which they are a part", and has summarized the sociological aspect of reference group theory. Men frequently orient themselves to groups other than their own in shaping their behaviour and evaluation. In general, reference group theory aims to systematize the determinants and consequences of those processes of evaluation and self-appraisal in which the individual takes the values and standards of other individuals and groups as a comparative frame of reference" (Merton, 1968: 234).

The reference group may be of (a) imitation type, (b) identification type and (c) negative reference; in the case of imitation type of reference group; the ways of behaviour are accepted as right and proper or as useful and therefore is imitated by the other group making the reference. Marton (1968) says that non-membership groups are likely to be adopted as reference groups in those social systems, which have high rates of social mobility and open than those which are relatively closed. Thus, non-membership groups are not likely to be adopted as positive reference groups in relatively closed societies. As a result, members of the lower stratum are not likely to adopt higher stratum as a reference group and cannot be a source of mobility in such societies (Fishbein, 1973: 271-286). Thus, India becomes such a case in point. Logically, in the closed society, non-membership groups should not be adopted as positive reference groups, i.e. to say that members of the lower social stratum are not likely to adopt higher stratum as their positive reference group. But according to Alexander (1968: 3-9), non-membership groups have different kinds of orientations towards groups depending upon their closed or open character. Alexander condemns Merton by stating that in closed societies reference groups behaviour or anticipatory socialization may take place and such behaviour may have functional consequence. A member may take members of his own group as his ideal or role model, as they have made greater achievements. In such a situation, the reference group becomes one's own membership group.

The process of imitation on the part of lower groups has become more complex in contemporary India. There are multiple reference groups and there is further compact neutralization that occurs in reference groups (Parvathamma, 1973: 6). Thus, there is a possibility of understanding the behaviour patterns of the women leaders by the concept of reference groups in the sense to whom they consider as their role models.

The women leaders have considered some persons of their groups and also from among other social groups as their models in becoming leaders. To whom within their own group or outside in non-membership group, they consider as their positive reference models (groups). In the process of becoming leaders, they might have discarded some persons or groups to whom they dislike, would be understood as their negative reference models. In the first category, leader like late Dr. Ambedkar is likely to be the positive reference model for his own caste people. The other higher caste persons may also be their positive reference groups (models). The same positive reference models may be followed in performing their roles as leaders.

1.7.8 *Development*

Development is here used to mean both the improved material well being (welfare) of people and the process by which this improved well being is achieved. The concept of development also includes an element of equality that material benefits from the development process should be fairly distributed, especially benefit to those most in need — the disadvantaged and the most vulnerable. Therefore, the special interest in women's development arises because women are a majority amongst the most disadvantaged (Longwe, 1996: 3).

1.7.9 *Empowerment*

Empowerment is an important element of development, being the process by which people take control and action in order to overcome obstacles. Empowerment especially means the collective action by the oppressed and deprived to overcome the obstacles of structural inequality which have previously put them in a disadvantaged position. The women's empowerment framework sees empowerment as the goal and the essential process for women's advancement. It is the process by which women mobilize to understand, identify and overcome gender discrimination, so as to achieve equality of welfare and equal access to resources. Empowerment may be analytically distinguished from "self-reliance", which may be defined as people's ability to advance themselves within the existing social system (ibid: 1996).

1.7.10 *Gender Awareness*

Gender awareness means the ability to identify problems arising from gender inequality and indiscrimination, even if these are not very evident on the surface, or are "hidden" — are not part of the general or commonly accepted explanation of what and where the problem lies. In other words, gender awareness means a high level of gender conscintization (ibid: 1996).

1.7.11 *Gender Discrimination*

Gender discrimination means to give differential treatment to individuals on the grounds of their gender. In a patriarchal society, this involves systematic and structural discrimination against women in the distribution of income, access to resources and participation in decision making (ibid: 1996).

1.7.12 *Gender Equality*

Gender equality means that there is no discrimination on grounds of a person's sex in the allocation of resources or benefits, or in the access to services. Gender equality may be measured in terms of whether there is equality of opportunity, or equality of results. The *UN Convention on the Elimination of All Forms of Discrimination Against Women* can be understood as a statement on what the principle of gender equality of opportunity should mean in practice for all aspects of life, and all sectors of the economy, (ibid: 3).

1.7.13 *Gender Equity*

It means fairness and justice in the distribution of benefits and responsibilities between the two genders. Gender equality does not have such a well-defined meaning as gender equal opportunity, because its meaning depends on the definition of fairness and justice. In addition, in its legal sense the term equity suggests a limited notion of the concept of justice, since equity refers to justice within the existing law, rather than justice by changing the law. By contrast, the women's empowerment framework follows the 1979 Women's Convention in defining justice for women in terms of gender equality. The lack of definition in terms of equity has led to the word being used in quite different ways. It can be used as a "stronger" word than equality by those who recognize that woman must demand more than equality with man in a man's world, and that gender equality must also entail the transformation to be a different and more just society. On the other hand, those who wish to avoid awkward issues can sometimes use equity as a weak euphemism for equality (ibid: 3).

2

AN OVERVIEW OF LITERATURE

This chapter provides a brief survey of select literature that is divided in two parts. The first part takes note of the conditions of women in a historical perspective and the second part presents the trend of studies on leadership in general and women leaders in particular.

2.1 Women Through Ages

Almost half of mankind is really womankind. This half, in every age and every land, has coexisted with men in a relationship, which has varied between complete submission and complete equality. To men, women have been "fair sex", "better half' and "weaker sex" but they had no scruples in evolving a society, which was usually maledominated. In history, women suffered from natural and imposed handicaps and yet, in all ages, some of them ably projected themselves and acquired the position of leadership and authority (Bhatt, 1995:11). No field of human endeavour remained untouched by them and the contribution made by them was substantial and significant. Even now, women account for two-thirds of the world's work hours. They produce 60 to 80 per cent of the food in Africa and Asia, 40 per cent in Latin America. Yet they officially constitute only one-third of the world's labour force, receive only 10 per cent of its income and own less than one per cent of its prosperity. The work done by women in the home and on the farm is never calculated into the gross national product of any country. Their unpaid contributions to their nation's economies have largely been overlooked (Helmore, 1985 : 1).

"The chief of the *United Nations Development Fund for Women (UNDFW)*, Margaret Snyder, has aptly said that women are the providers of food, fuel, water, and often the whole family income;

the sustainers and developers of their families, communities, and countries" (ibid: 2).

Julius Nyerere, the retired President of Tanzania summed up the problem succinctly:

> *A person does not walk very far or very fast on one leg. How can we expect half the people to be able to develop a nation ? Yet the reality is that women are usually left aside when development needs are discussed* (ibid.-2).

Shirley Williams (1978), president of the Social Democratic Party of Britain, has observed that:

> *Curiously enough, considering that in many ways women are more equal in the (United) States, it is more common to find women in high places in Europe and Asia than in America* (Williams, 1987: 28).

The tradition in the old and established societies of Europe and Asia (including India) has permitted women to have their own role in the past — a role, which may even entail the right to command. No such tradition exists in America, Australia, Canada and other new societies, which grew in one-time "colonies". The British politician further observed:

> *I don't think that there will be, at least in this millennium, an American woman President. There may just possibly be an American Vice President* (ibid: 31).

So here is a paradox. New societies, like that of the USA, have succeeded in establishing the equality of sexes but have failed to throw up women Presidents, Prime Ministers and other women in commanding position in political life. Older societies in Europe and Asia may not have achieved equality of women with men to the desirable extent, but they have propelled to power, through their political processes, women leaders like Margaret Thatcher, Corazon Aquino, Bandarnaike and Indira Gandhi.

If the institution of monarchy brought forth Queen Elizabeth I, Catherine the Great or Queen Victoria in Europe, it also brought forth Sultana Razia Begam, Maharani Durgawati and Maharani

Ahalyabai Holkar in India. If national perils and calamities brought forth women trailblazers like Joan de Arc and Florence Nightingale in Europe, they also brought to prominence women leaders like Chand Bibi and Sister Nivedita in this country. Cleopatra and Madam de Pompadour had their prototypes on the Indian scene also (Bhatt, 1995:13).

The question of women's role all through the history is thus intimately bound up with historical epochs dating from the early cultures of at least 4000 years ago. The discovery of the Indus Valley civilization in the 20th century bears out the settled nature of the peaceful people who lived around 3500 B.C. like the other societies (ibid: 1995:13).

Going back to the hoary past of the Vedic period about 2500 B.C., women occupied a high status in society and gave evidence of their creative talent, which was no less than that of men. Many gifted women composed sacred hymns, which were included in the Rigveda, the earliest work of literature in the world (Bhatt, 1995:14).

The *Rigveda* reveals how women took a prominent part in the Vedic rituals because of their talent in music, which they learnt as a part of their education. It mentions that women sang on ceremonial occasions and played on a variety of rare instruments, such as the 'vina', the 'kanda vina', the 'taluka vina' as well as flutes and drums.

Ahalya, Sita, Draupadi, Mandodari and Tara were the names of great women, each of different hue and each with her own eminence. How well they anticipate — one wonders did they inspire? Manu the lawgiver's dictum:

> *Let the names of women be good to pronounce — sweet, simple, pleasant and appropriate, let them terminate in long vowels and resemble words of benediction* (Jain, 1975:51).

These five women, widely known as *Panchkanyan*, were neither saints nor virgins. None of them was heavenly; they were wives and mothers but they represented the colourful variety of their qualities. In the period of the Upanishads, Maitreyi and her daughter Gargi were prominent philosophers and both distinguished themselves in the art of rhetoric. The *Mahabharata* of the epic period makes mention of Uttara, daughter of King Virata and her companions who were adept in dancing, singing and instrumental music, while Madhvi, daughter of King Yayati, was an expert musician. In one of the early Indian epics, Princess Usha's maid of honour, Chitralekha, was a portrait painter of great talent who sketched the portrait of the noble men of her time to help identify Aniruddha, the grandson of Sri Krishna (ibid: 51).

Muslim rule in India produced many distinguished women, including Razia Begum, who was prudent and capable daughter of Iltutmish, Sultan of Delhi. He is supposed to have said: "My sons are devoted to the pleasures of youth and none of them is qualified to be a king... there is no one else competent to guide the state than my daughter." Razia's military and administrative leadership was superb. But in a male dominated society, she had been born too soon and found herself in a web of intrigues and revolts. Her reign was, therefore, short and she was murdered in 1240 A.D. Rani Durgawati is famous for her heroic resistance to expansionist drive of Akbar, the Great Mughal. How she bravely faced his vast armies with her small army of 500 men will ever be remembered and retold with pride for generations to come. Rani Durgawati fell fighting against Akbar's forces in 1564. The poetess daughter of Baber, Gulbadan Begum, immortalized her name by writing the Humayun Namah, a valuable contemporary record in beautiful write-up with style of the text of the life of the Emperor and his family in 16th century (Bharatiya Vidhya Bhavan, 1974: 633).

Nur Jahan (1574-1646), which means the light of the world, was brilliant and beautiful wife of Emperor Jahangir. She was blessed with great artistic, intellectual and administrative talent. A rare tribute was paid to her in a Persian couplet, which runs: "Though Nur Jahan is apparently a woman yet, in the ranks of the brave, she is the (only) tamer of the lion" (Baig, 1958: 169).

Chand Bibi was the caretaker of the infant King Bahadur in Ahmednagar and died fighting the Mughals setting an example of bravery and courage. Jahanara Begum (1613-1683 A.D.), talented daughter of Emperor Shah Jahan, took great interest in both architecture and decorative gardens. Zebunnisa, the accomplished daughter of Emperor Aurangzeb, possessed great skill in calligraphy and wrote elegant verses of rare beauty under the pen name of 'Makhfi', which have been collected in the volume, Diwan-i-Makhfi. Tara Bai emerged as a prudent woman when Marathas were constantly fighting against the Mughals. She, being a lady of masterly spirit, guided the destiny of the Maratha nation at a very juncture as the regent for her minor son, Shivaji III. After the death of Mohan Rao Holkar, his widow Ahalya Bai became the head of the administration and became a historical personage in her own right (ibid: 170).

The position that women occupied in Hindu society at the dawn of civilization during the Vedic age was much better than what we ordinarily expect it to have been. During the age of *Rigveda* (from 2500 to 1500 B.C.), the position of women was fairly satisfactory. Ordinarily, girls were, no doubt, less welcome than boys, but it must be added that there were also some parents in society who would perform special religious rituals for the good luck of getting learned and capable daughters.

Girls were educated like boys and had to pass through a period of Brahmcharya. The marriages of girls used to take place at a fairly advanced age, the normal time being the age of 16 or 17. Women had an absolute equality with men in the eyes of religion. The position of the wife was an honoured one in the family. If a wife had the misfortune to be widowed, she had not to ascend her husband's funeral pyre. The custom of Sati was not in vogue at all; on the contrary, widow remarriage was permitted. However, the main disabilities from which women suffered in this age, as well as in the next one, were proprietary ones. They could hold or inherit no property. Otherwise, the community allowed them considerable freedom in the different activities of social and political life (Bhatt, 1995:14).

In the age of later Samhitas, Brahmanas and Upanishads (1500 to 500 B.C.), changes which took place in the position of women were rather gradual. Their proprietary rights continued to be unrecognized. There was, however, a gradual decline in female education as times advanced. The system of sending out girls to renowned gurus or centres of education came to be discouraged.

As a consequence, there arose a tendency to curtail the religious rights and privileges of the average women. The ideals pertaining to marriage and mutual relations and rights of parties continued to be more or less the same as they were in the earlier age. The custom of Sati was altogether unknown, and the widow had the option of remarriage either to her brother-in-law or to another person (ibid : 19).

Down to 500 A.D., permission was granted to child widows to remarry. From about 1,000 A.D., no widow in a respectable family could remarry whatever her age might have been at the time of her husband's death. The prohibition of widow remarriage came to be regarded as the most important criterion of the respectability of a class both high and low down to the beginning of the present century. The prejudice against widow remarriage was so deep rooted that the legislation permitting widow remarriage, passed in 1856 A.D., had no appreciable effect on the situation for more than half a century (ibid: 19).

Down to about 800 A.D., Smritis were emphatic in declaring that women, who were forcibly taken into captivity or dishonoured, should be admitted back to their families. An outsider like Alberuni could not understand the stupidity of the Hindu community in refusing to readmit men and women, who had been captured and converted by force. From 1200 A.D., Hindu society refused to follow the lead of Smriti writers and declared that once a woman was converted or taken into captivity, nothing would justify her readmission to her old family and religion. This rigid and unreasonable attitude has cost Hindu society very dearly.

The survey of the position of Hindu women reveals that there has been a constant decline in the status and condition of women during the last two thousand years. It is, no doubt, true that women, as a general rule, received similar and often worse treatment in contemporary times in several other civilizations both in the East and the West. There are some evidences also which prove that the average woman during the last two thousand years continued to lead a happy and contented life but her cup of happiness was more frequently spoiled in this period than ever before.

Even today, in spite of independence, good legislation,

education of women and reduction of illiteracy, many social evils and customs exist in Indian society. Indian women on the whole never sought to sublimate or rationalize her limitation and disabilities or bypass family life. However, hard and even be cruel to her. On the contrary, their homes and families have invariably come first in their order of priority. This has the very important result, however, of maintaining a stable and integrated society (ibid : 22).

Status, in pure sociological terms, denotes only the position *vis-a-vis* others in terms of rights and obligations. In discussions on women's status in any society, the general convention has been to assess their role in relation to men. Two other dimensions have been introduced in the recent times to facilitate such assessment, particularly in a period of process of change: (a) the extent of actual control enjoyed by women over their own lives; (b) the extent to which they have access to decision making processes and are effective in positions of power and authority.

While the politico-legal framework of a society indicates the scope of rights and obligations of its members, the advent of quantitative methods has made it possible to adopt certain statistical indicators, e.g., literacy and education, employment and political participation, age of marriage and other demographic features that may help to locate the status of women *vis-a-vis* men, both at a given point of time, as well as to measure the extent of change over a period. But the application of these indicators to a society like India poses several problems such as cultural variations, social hierarchy, economic inequality and secular law. Rendering the two-dimensional formula is neither quite relevant nor effective in assessing their role. Similarly, woman's roles, right and norms of behaviour are greatly influenced by cultural factors like the institution of family, kinship, groups, descent systems, religious and other cultural traditions, caste hierarchy, etc. The process of social change, development and modernization, impact of alien and western culture, which are sometimes complementary, sometimes contradictory and destructive of each other, are also involved in making any worthwhile assessment (ibid: 23-24).

Appreciation of this complexity led the Committee on the Status of Women in India to admit that

> *"The status of women in Indian context cannot be defined simply by general concepts like equality, role-differentiation, legal, social and political rights, depending or independence are not applicable to all sections of our population. How do we then assess the status of Indian women, or measure the degree or direction of change in their position? Against the new dimensions in women's status and roles introduced by the constitution and process of social change, this large section of our society still continues to be under the influence of traditional standards. Traditional India has seen a woman only as a member of the family or a group as daughter, wife and mother and not as an individual with an identity or rights of her own. The radicalism of the constitution and its deliberate departure from inherited social system lay in its implicit assumption that every adult woman, whatever her social position or accomplishments, will function the task of nation building"* (Ministry of Education and Social Welfare, 1975:7).

The social movements spearheaded by Arya Samaj, Brahmo Samaj, Ramakrishna Mission, etc., which began in 19th century, emphasized enhancement of women's status through education, restriction of child marriage, improvement in the condition of widows and provision of property rights for Hindu women and widows. While the reformers were certainly concerned with the oppressed conditions of women and were interested in improving their lot through legislation and arousing of social conscience; very few of them thought in terms of women's rights to participate in social functions outside the framework of the family.

Mahatma Gandhi believed that the freedom movement, to be successful, had to be a movement of the masses. He felt that "Swaraj" would be meaningless without the reform of the social structure and the upliftment of the weaker sections, namely, the women and the lower social strata to a position of equality with others. While lending his support to the cause of improving women's conditions through education and reform of marriage laws, he declared himself to be uncompromising in the matter of women's rights. He wrote:

> *Woman has been suppressed under custom and law for which man was responsible and in the shaping of which she had no hand. Woman has as much right to shape her own destiny as man has to shape his. It is upto man to see that they enable them to realise their full status and play their part as equal of men* (*Young India*, 7h October, 1921).

Mahatma Gandhi insisted that they must play an equal role with men in the achievement of freedom and social justice. In his opinion women had natural abilities to lead a non-violent struggle for human liberation. The most significant aspect of Gandhi's ideas lies in the remarkable similarities between them and the demands which are now being voiced by the women's liberation movements all over the world; equality in family and society, the right of one's own-body, the opening of wider opportunities for self-development and a refusal to be regarded merely as sex symbols.

Though the implications of Gandhian social philosophy were not fully realized at that time, the massive participation of women in the freedom struggle resulted in transformation of women's position in the eyes of society. As President of the Indian National Congress in 1931, Jawaharlal Nehru accepted equal obligations along with equal rights in the Fundamental Rights Resolution passed by the Congress in that year. Along with adult suffrage, the resolution emphasized the need for protection of women workers and grant of maternity leave to them.

Nehru held that women "must" be trained to participate "in every department of human activity" and play an active part in all professions and spheres. For this purpose, they must fight social institutions like purdah, untouchability, caste, marriage laws and customs that crushed them. But above all, they must participate in a struggle against the root cause of evils. A direct result of the "merging" of the women's movement with the national political struggle was the rejection of all suggestions for political reservations for women in legislative bodies on the same lines as adopted for other weaker sections of society. Women leaders, who had functioned as equals of their male comrades in the freedom movement, decided that absolute equality in the political process would be the ideal remedy to raise women's status in society.

As a result of the commitment made by the Congress as early as 1931, the equality clauses were passed by the Constituent Assembly without any debate or discussion. This was, however, disapproved by the sharp controversy in the same body on the question of reform of Hindu law relating to marriage and inheritance. The suggestions for a reform of Hindu Law had in fact come from the reform movement, and the women's movement in particular, in the pre-independence period. Even those who framed the Constitution had not seriously appreciated equality clauses in the Constitution. After years of debate and considerable modifications, the law could be enacted only piecemeal in the mid-fifties.

As a result of these laws, the legal position of Hindu women has improved considerably. These laws include the ban on bigamy, the provision of right of divorce and right to inherit a share of parental property. While legal reform has improved considerably the status of Hindu women, similar reforms have not taken place in all the other systems of personal law prevalent in India.

Apart from these, free India has adopted a series of social laws for the control and eradication of certain social practices, such as dowry and immoral traffic in women, as they degrade the status of women. Labour laws adopted on the lines of ILO Convention have sought to protect the health of women workers and ensure for them humane working conditions. The equal Remuneration Convention of the ILO, though ratified by the Government of India some years earlier, has been given a legal shape in the form of an ordinance in 1975 (Phadinis, Urmilla and Malini, 1978: 23). Judging by the standards of many developing and even developed countries, the legal and political rights conferred on women in India would thus appear to be considerably high. When one compares them with the situation that prevailed at the beginning of the 20th century, the progress may even appear fantastic.

The spread of education and access to positions of influence and power in the profession and in Government will undoubtedly open enormous opportunities to women to develop their talent and to participate in all the spheres of activities, competing with men on equal terms. Women have now gatecrashed into hitherto close professions like engineering, architecture, business management and public administration, political and diplomatic representation, and all branches of higher education and scientific research. In all these fields they have been accepted at present on their merits.

2.2 Constitutional Provisions

The Constitution of India, implemented in 1950, carried the impact of reforms enacted since the middle of 19th century and demands made during the freedom struggle for women's development. Article 15(3) under 'Fundamental Rights' reads, "Nothing in this article shall prevent the State from making special provision for women and children". Article 16(1) guarantees "equality of opportunity for all citizens in matters relating to employment for appointment to any office under the State", and Article 16(2) forbids discrimination "in respect of any employment of office under the State" on the grounds of "religion, race, caste, sex, descent, place of birth, residence or any of them".

Part IV of the Constitution deals with the Directive Principles of State Policy (Articles 36 to 51). Some of the Directive Principles are 'women-specific'. Others concern women directly or by implication. Among those, which concern women directly and have a special bearing on their status, are the following:

1. The State is required to "direct its policy towards securing" : That the citizens, men and women equally have the right to an adequate means of livelihood — *Article 39(a);*
2. That there is equal pay for equal work for both men and women — *Article 39(d);*
3. That the health and strength of workers, men and women, are not abused — *Article 39(e);* and
4. The State is also required to make provision for securing just and human conditions of work and for maternity benefits— *Article 42.*

In addition, Article 44 states, "The State shall endeavour to secure for the citizens a uniform civil code throughout the territory of India". This is significantly in the context of the personal laws with the people of different religions follow in matters of marriage, succession and property rights. Not all of them have been pro-women, however.

2.3 Supplementary Legislations

Despite these provisions, or possibly to reinforce them and empower women, the Indian Parliament passed various legislations in the field of family, marriage, property, inheritance, etc. so that women could be integrated in the development process and equality brought about. Such integration alone would help women to participate equally in the public and political sphere.

Social legislations, numbering more than 30, deal with important areas; some of them are as follows:

1. Hindu Marriage Act, 1955 and Special Marriage Act, 1954;
2. Hindu Adoptions and Maintenance Act, 1956;
3. Suppression of Immoral Traffic in Women and Girls Act, 1956;
4. The Hindu Minority and Guardianship Act, 1956;
5. The Hindu Succession Act, 1956;
6. The Christian Matrimonial Causes Bill, 1960;
7. The Maternity Benefit Act, 1961;
8. The Dowry Prohibition Act, 1961;
9. Indian Foreign Service (Conduct and Discipline) Rules, 1961;
10. The Factories Act, 1948; The Factories (Amendment) Act, 1976; Mines Act, 1952; and Plantation Labour Act, 1951;
11. Bidi and Cigar Workers (Conditions of Service) Act, 1966;
12. Medical Termination of Pregnancy Act, 1971;
13. The Adoption of Children's Bill, 1972;
14. The Equal Remuneration Act, 1976;
15. The Child Marriage Restraint (Amendment) Act, 1976;
16. Marriage Law (Amendment) Act, 1976;

17. Criminal Law (Amendment) Bill;
18. Marriage Law Amendment Bill, 1981;
19. Criminal Law (Second Amendment) Act, 1983;
20. The Hindu Widows Remarriage (Repeat) Act, 1986;
21. The Family Courts Act, 1984;
22. The Indecent Representation of Women (Prohibition) Act, 1986 ;
23. Muslim Women (Protection of Rights on Divorce) Act, 1986;
24. Commission of Sati (Prevention) Act, 1987; and
25. Crimes Against Women and Girls in the name of Religion or Custom (Prevention and Abolition) Act, 1987.

As equal citizens of India, women benefit from these rights equally with men. However, since the Constitution recognized the unequal social position of women, a special clause empowers the State to make special provisions for women. This poser has been used to enact special laws for the protection of women workers in factories, mines and plantation and to provide maternity relief to women workers in the organized sector.

Article 16 guarantees equality of opportunity in public employment and office under the State. This clause has helped to ensure a significant position and status to the Indian women, which is demonstrated in the increasing number of women in the public services and in positions of political power and dignity including such top offices as Governor, Chief Minister and Prime Minister.

The Directive Principles of State Policy defining the major goals of a Welfare State also contain specific items affecting women. The special attention given to the needs and problems of women as one of the "weaker sections" of Indian society, and the recognition of political equality was undoubtedly a radical departure from the norms prevailing in traditional India of pre-independence days. It has led many scholars to describe the Indian Constitution as a manifesto of a social revolution. This has to be understood in the historical setting of the Indian freedom movement and the decision taken by the Indian National Congress, under the leadership of Mahatma Gandhi, to ensure legal and political equality for women.

2.4 Employment of Women

Turning to the sphere of employment, generally considered as an important indicator of women's status, one finds several contradictory trends. The organised sector of the economy, i.e. in services and professions and that sector of industry which may be described as the creation of the 20th century, the employment of women has increased fairly rapidly in the years since independence, at a rate faster than the growth rate in total employment for this sector. This sector, however, indicates a very small minority of the women workers in this country.

Agriculture still continues to provide livelihood to the largest masses of women in India and has absorbed an increasing proportion of women workers with the decline of opportunities in traditional industries and services. As a result, the decline in the absolute number of women workers in agriculture has been less precipitate, from 30.8 million in 1911 to 25 million in 1971. In 1971 the number of women cultivators had dropped to 9.2 million while that of agriculture labourers were increased to 15.7 million. Commenting on this transformation, the Committee on the Status of Women in India observed that this "is the greatest indicator of increasing poverty employment and not of improving rights and opportunities for economic participation" (Ministry of Education and Social Welfare: 1975).

While a trend towards equalization of wages between men and women has been visible in the organized sector, discrimination against women is quite apparent in various ways in the rule throughout agriculture and the rest of the organized sector. Since 94 per cent of women workers are engaged in the unorganized sector of the economy (81 per cent in agriculture) they are unaffected by the protection afforded by the Labour Laws, and are victims of low productivity, unemployment and underemployment. According to estimates of various Expert Committees women constitute the larger share of both the unemployment and underemployment in India.

In the face of these demographic trends, the *Committee on the Status of Women in India* was compelled to conclude that the continuing decline in the sex ratio and the higher mortality rate of women was primarily due to worsening conditions of life of women in the poorer sections of society. While education, legal rights and changing social attitudes have opened new vistas for the active participation in all spheres of life to a minority of women in the privileged sections, the conditions of women among the vast masses of the population lower down have not shown similar improvement but have, on the other hand, registered a decline at least in the economic sphere.

It concedes that women in India have been deprived of power within the family by mainstream religious and social traditions. They have been powerless over their own lives because of forced subservience to fathers, husbands and in-laws, as also due to violence within the family and limited educational opportunities. They have lived in a social set up in which power and authority in both domestic and political spheres have been "built around a hierarchy of males" (Jain, 1984: 1790). There have been many cultural barriers to women's equality, which are outside the realm of government action.

The UNESCO Survey revealed in 1989 that there were more women in medicine, education, science, technology and law in India than in the western countries. The same survey pointed out that in the city of Delhi, the number of women graduates exceeded the number of men graduates (ibid: 33). It is no small wonder that women have created some measure of political influence for themselves within the electoral system of India. The political presence of women has made a significant impact on federal, state and local politics. News headlines have been telling us about the exploits of the women guerrillas of the Naxalite movement and the courage of female nurses in wartime hospitals.

One by one, the male bastions (like aeronautics) are falling before the onslaught of the skilled Indian women of the 20th century. They have so far been excluded from the Indian defence forces and their combat units (there are 220,000 military women in the U.S.). Recently, Indian military establishment has now opened at least half a door for them. But they are conspicuous in police services and, since February 1986, in the Central Reserve Police

Force (CRPF) whose *Mahila Battalion* is the first women's para-military force in Asia, its members have handled Meerut riots and performed police duties in Sri Lanka (as part of IPKF) and Kashmir (Bhatt, 1993: 34). Thus, women in India have marked their presence in occupations and professions, which were hitherto male dominated.

2.5 Women in Politics

The participation of women in Indian politics can be traced in many ways. The freedom struggle in India is one of the few liberation movements in the world, which witnessed a vast participation by women. The extent, nature and method of this participation broadly followed the pattern of the evolution and growth of the Indian national movement as a whole.

Sixty years of the movement witnessed the beginning and gradual growth of women's participation. There was formal, direct and visible participation of women in various activities like singing, writing, partaking in protests, processions, going to jail, etc. and in the more peaceful forms of *satyagraha* and non-violent non-cooperation. Many women even took up training in gun carrying. And there was an informal process of participation such as lending support and backing up with various activities, which have not always been singled out.

The presence and contribution of the women, however, were recognised by the leaders, particularly during the era of Gandhi's leadership. At the same time, the absence of a separate women's selection in the movement meant that the various organisations pursuing the interests of women had to act on their own; they also served as pressure groups both on the British rule and on the Indian National Movement. Many women served in both, establishing a link between the two. By the beginning of the twentieth century, many women's organisations working specifically on women's issues were born. Women's education, health, training colleges for women, construction of homes for widows, scholarships, medical colleges and short maternity courses for women, etc. were some of the issues women's organisations were concerned about. They also recognised quickly that the emancipation was inextricably linked to the political freedom of the nation. The various organisations, dealing with the multifarious problems and activities of women, had to be brought together and amalgamated, if women's questions had to be highlighted and their emancipation achieved. It was with this in view that the All India Women's Conference was created in October 1926. Many women believed that their rights and issues could not be secured in isolation from nationalist struggle (Kaushik, 1996: 53-81).

The mobilization of women in large numbers weakened the bondage of tradition and encouraged them to develop a perspective on the wider socio-political problems. Their close links with the national movement helped them acquire the right to political participation, to franchise and to other constitutional rights. Women occupying various positions, both in the political and professional spheres, began to be tacitly accepted. With this legacy of large-scale participation in national politics, women in independent India participated as free and equal citizens. This participation can be analyzed in its various domains.

2.5.1 *Participation in Electoral Politics*

The participation of women in the electoral process is an indicator of their political consciousness as well as their aspiration for status enhancement. A quick glance at women's participation in elections over the past three decades and twelfth and thirteenth general elections will confirm the initial hopes placed in them. The figures concerning women's formal participation in the electoral process, both as actors and objects of attention, bring out a few facts: (i) the extent, nature and level of Indian women's participation is much greater than in many other countries; (ii) this participation has been more or less steadily expanding over the years through various elections — as voters, as candidates and in terms of participation in campaigning; (iii) the gap in the turnout between the men and women is increasingly narrowing down; and (iv) the number of women getting elected to representative bodies is steadily increasing (Kaushik, 1993: 53-81).

2.5.2 *Women's Participation in the Grassroots Democracy*

Democracy and development, in order to be successful, need the maximum participation of people at the lowest level. Panchayati Raj (democratic decentralization) is an important political innovation and a vital conduit in India, for popular participation in democratic development. It is envisaged not merely as a method of implementation of rural development policies and the dispersal of developmental benefits, but more importantly, as the training ground for the promotion of local initiative for increasing people's political consciousness, their awareness of their rights and for their direct participation in self-rule. Panchayati Raj being the best and most widespread training ground for the emergence of Indian leadership, the question of women's participation becomes all the more vital. With this in view, as early as 1962, many state governments like Andhra Pradesh and Maharashtra initiated Panchayati Raj reorganization wherein they had specially stipulated the representation of women.

The inclusion of women, by co-option and nomination if necessary, in the elected bodies, it was believed, would lead to their greater participation in the local political processes and thereby promote their development through empowerment. Even though the experiment had not proved totally satisfactory, partly due to the small number of women involved and partly due to a lack of political consciousness, the *Gram Panchayats* and *Mahila Mandals* have been performing their roles moderately and working as a training ground. The whole experiment is considered conducive, in the long run, to the process of democratic decentralization wherein political power can be devolved to women (Kaushik, 1993: 53-81).

2.5.3 *Women in Trade Union Movements in India*

The participation of women in the trade unions, however, is far from satisfactory. It is primarily due to the nature of women's work and also due to the trade unions' ways of functioning. But this is also the result of a strong patriarchal attitude prevalent among the workers and their leaders. Besides, trade unions cover mainly the organized sector and much of women's work falls under the unorganized sector.

This is so despite the fact that many women have been active participants in the trade union movements. There are women workers who have evinced a great deal of interest and shown loyalty to trade union activities. In fact, Anusuyaben Sarabhai founded the first trade union in India (of textile mill workers) in Ahemedabad in 1917. In general, she remained its President until her death. The patriarchal attitude of the male workers and their leaders appear to be responsible for poor representation of women in decision-making positions and the neglect of issues concerning women. Many male workers view their female counterparts as basically homemakers (ibid: 53-81).

It is only in recent times that the three major trade unions, namely, INTUC, AITUC and CITU, have begun paying attention to women workers. At the same time, women workers have started struggling on their own, seeking to fulfil demands that concern them as women. This has not always been successful, but many a time their firmness as well as the support received from active women's groups, have paid dividends. However, even in these movements (except where they are made up exclusively of women members) they have not been able to emerge beyond middle level leadership, despite their commitment and militancy.

2.5.4 *Participation in Peasant Movement in India*

Women form the bulk of agricultural labour in India. The history of agrarian movements shows that women had participated in great numbers. Women participants had fled from home and lived without food and endured all kinds of hardships. During the Avadh Movement of 1920-21, women had been mobilized on a large scale. The Kisan Sabha movements under Sahajananda saw a wide participation of women. They surrounded fields of grain, *gheraoed* the authorities and organized the fighting (ibid: 53-81).

The *Tebhaga Movement* (1946-50) in Bengal witnessed the rise of women's group called '*Nari Bahini*'. What motivated them were women's issues such as wife beating and rape by *Zamindars* (landlords). They represented cases of violence and molestation in people's courts. They raised questions of sexual division of labour and control over income. Despite violence, rape and killing, women participated fearlessly to maintain the communication network and shelter the activities (ibid: 53-81).

The Telengana Movement (1946-51) was another peasant struggle in which women participated in guerrilla tactics and played leadership roles, facing torture, molestation and repression by the police and Razakars in the process. Women also mobilized themselves against child marriage, concubinage and dowry (ibid: 53-81).

However, the impact of women's participation on the peasant movement itself is not very discernible. Issues of agricultural labour like minimum wages or equal pay for equal work are not enforced or even strongly demanded. Women continue to be the victims of gender violence, with very little protest. They do not figure as objects in land reforms. With a major chunk of rural households consisting of subsistence farmers and with an increasing number of female-headed households owing to the migration of male members to towns, women who actually cultivate are increasing in numbers. But it is the man who owns the land and makes the decisions. Peasant and agricultural labour struggles do not seem to recognize the valuable participation and role of women.

The above analysis shows the present position and trends of women's participation in the formal political processes in India. Compared to many developed and developing countries, Indian trends are positive and optimistic. But by itself, and when compared to its population, women's participation in politics is still very low, and in any case much lower than men. If one has to gauge how ordinary women perceive their realm of politics, what their goals and strategies are and where they derive their power from, one will have to give up conventional methodologies of finding answers to such questions like how many women got elected to public offices or how they dominate political parties. There is a need to evolve some alternate ways to assess women's participation in politics.

Such a study must deal with the thousands of 'ordinary women' rather than the view 'superwomen' and their 'achievements'; it should pursue the ordinary women's ways of empowering themselves in order to 'fit' political institutions to their needs and purposes.

2.6 Trend of Studies on Women Politicians/Leaders

Four major kinds of writings exist on 'women in politics'. Of these, a good number are in the form of seminar papers, mostly unpublished and not widely circulated, with the bulk being made up of papers presented in the four national conferences of the Indian Association for Women's Studies, conference of Organization of Social Scientists, seminars conducted by different universities, colleges, research institutes and other NGOs (ibid: 53-81). There are also M.A., M.Phil. and Ph.D. dissertations and reports. The S.N.D.T. Women's University, Bombay, the Women's Studies and Development Centre, University of Delhi and Documentation Centres of I.C.S.S.R. have compiled comprehensive lists on women's studies (ibid: 53-81).

Another set of material is the books and articles published by commercial publishers, research institutions, universities and NGOs. Of late, interest in such publications has grown. Among them 'Kali' and 'Shakti' are especially devoted to books on women. A few journals (*Economic and Political Weekly, Mainstream, Lokayan Bulletin, Teaching Politics*) regularly carry academic articles on women. *Samya Shakti* is a journal devoted exclusively to research-based women's studies. So, too, is *Manushi*, which publishes articles and features based on actual experiences. Then there are newsletters, Bulletins and occasional monographs from social action groups (*Saheli, Chetna*, etc.), research institutions and universities, which among other things, present articles, features and data on women's participation in politics.

Finally, there are government documents in the form of reports, policy statements, schemes and programmes. Some of them do go beyond policies and throw light on women's actual participation. The Report of the Committee on Status of Women (1976) was the first and till today the most important document on the women's participation in the socio-economic and political life in the country. As a pioneering venture, it put together under one cover data analysis on different aspects of women's lives and social participation. This was done after considerable research, many field visits and personal interviews. Though outdated in terms of figures and some of its recommendations, the report is still valid in terms of its analysis. Particular significance is its stress on the values of equality and justice in the context of the Directive Principles of State Policy and Fundamental Rights of the Indian Constitution (ibid: 53-81).

It was followed by the reports of the Non-Aligned Conference on Women held in New Delhi in April 1985, which threw substantial light on women's position in the Third World, and particularly in India, and recommended a plan for action. Then came the country paper presented by India at the Conference at Nairobi in July 1985. Among other things, it also dwelt on political participation. But since it was a brief government paper, its coverage was skeleton and confined to election and administrative details.

There have been more publications of late, which have presented recent statistical data on demographic and socio-economic details on women and on their participation in the socio-economic and political activities of the nation. In addition, there are two detailed reports by committees formed by the Department of Women and Child Development. The first is the National Perspective Plan for Women (1988), which is in the nature of stock taking on the position and problems of women, on various government policies and programmes in different sectors as well as the recommendations for further programmes and policies. The other major document, entitled '*Shram Shakti*', a Report of the National Commission on Self-employed Women and Women in the Informal Sector, submitted in 1988. Even though initiated by the government, these documents have been written by academicians and social workers from universities and research institutions and others working for women's development (ibid: 53-81).

The literature available on women in politics in India, though may not be enormous, is still considerable. The themes/topics covered by it are the following:

1. Participation in the Freedom Struggle;
2. Constitutional and legislative measures and debates;
3. Participation of women in the political process in independent India :

   (a) Ideology, politics and political parties;
   (b) Electoral and party participation;
   (c) Local government and politics;
   (d) Trade union, peasant and other social movements;

4. Autonomous women's movements and women's organizations;
5. Informal processes — struggles within and outside the family, cultural and social process (ibid: 53-81).

Many of the accounts of the freedom movement are mainly in the realm of formal processes such as demonstrations, processions and marches, and peaceful acts of disobedience and '*satyagrahas*'. They highlight other modes of participation too, such as picketing liquor and foreign cloth shops and raising slogans or going into jails. Thus, these facts speak of the mass base among women with the Indian National Movement clearly represented. For source material, the accounts depend on the speeches and writings of important leaders such as M.K. Gandhi, Jawaharlal Nehru, Sarojini Naidu and Kamaladevi Chattopadhayaya. This was enlarged with documents from the archives, the collections of All India Women's Conference and other similar organizations. Many doctoral scholars and other researchers have also undertaken extensive interviews with leaders and surviving participants to supplement this information. In fact, this seems to be the latest trend in women's studies in India.

However, even while such studies highlight different modes of participation, they have yet to come to grips with some of its essential aspects such as the impact of the nationalist movement on the personality of common women, the aspirations and hopes it raised, the inspiration and motivations that prompted them to participate or be involved in the movement. Equally important are the factors that facilitated or hindered the participation of women—

factors that were rooted in cultural, religious, economic, geographical and, above all, patriarchal familial surroundings.

2.7 Leadership and Women Leaders

The social science scholars at different levels have undertaken a number of studies evaluating to political leaders. A few studies are presented here to indicate the kind of issues examined in these studies and also indicate relevant findings on the issues proposed in the present work.

"The elite theory in essence argues that whatever is the political system, it is the few capable who are ultimately responsible for decision making and implementation. Thus, the elite model divides society into the two parts: a ruling minority and the ruled majority" (Pant and Kumar, 1986: 5). Some authors have tried to relate class-model with elite model, by arguing that political elite is the most effective part of the ruling political class. However, this political class cannot be considered a class because, according to Marx, "society is divided into ruled and ruling classes on the basis of the relations of production, prevailing in a society". While the elite theory claims that personal qualities of individuals separate rulers from the ruled.

Various authors to support or oppose a political system have also used elite theory. Earlier elite theorists like Pareto and Mosea used the theory to criticize democratic and socialist systems. They wanted to propound a realistic and scientific theory regarding the nature of the ruling authority. Shumpeter, on the other hand, held that democracy grew along with capitalist economic system and the process in these capitalist and socialist economic systems were analogous. According to him, the will of the people is the product and not the motive power of the political process. Like market mechanism, in political process also politicians behave like entrepreneurs and formulate policies in the light of popular demands, then they try to sell them in competitive voters' markets; and masses are like consumers who have to give preference for any one of the given products (i.e. policy packages). Thus, for him elites in politics are like entrepreneurs in the economic field (Pant and Kumar, 1986: 5).

The elitist concept of democracy was supported and further developed by Anthony Downs (1957), Harold Lasswell (1950), Robert Dahl (1961) and Giovanni Sartre (1976). They developed the theory of plurality of elites to accommodate elites in various groups who try to defend the interests of its members.

"A great deal has changed in law as politics in the last forty years in India" (Beteille, 1992). The social structure of elites in India had undergone three major transformations in its long history. The three periods refer to pre-British period, British period and post-Independence period. During the pre-British period, the elite structure in the Indian society remained monarchical-feudal, based on principles of hierarchy and governed by the twin principles of loyalty and patronage. Thus, elites remained authoritarian and charismatic through out this period (Pant and Kumar, 1986: 1-7).

During the British regime, the traditional elites such as landlords and princes were patronized by the regime though the government reduced the power and influence of traditional elites considerably by introducing many institutions. The new elites during this phase emerged with the help of those very institutions, which were developed by British to consolidate their regime. Thus, introduction of such institutions as the judiciary to establish rule of law, modern system of education, development of science and technology, establishment of a new bureaucratic administration, etc. helped the emergence of a new national liberal elite. Though these modern institutions and the liberal values of equality, liberty, justice, etc. influenced the new national liberal elite, at the same time it wanted to preserve and continue its cultural heritage as well. In other words, it wanted to maintain a sort of continuity with the old elite, though it was fundamentally different from it in its origin and nature. Its role was not traditionally ascribed and, secondly, it was not paternalistic feudal. The majority of the new elite came from the new professions such as those of journalists, lawyers, social workers, etc. However, it is also true that the new elite had a very narrow social base as it mostly belonged to upper castes, and was more urban rather than rural (ibid: 1-7).

The country's elite structure changed further after Independence. As the competition to reach positions of power became open, regional, ethnic and linguistic interest groups appeared each claiming a share in the national cake. This emergence of new pressure groups widened the social base from which members of the elite came to be recruited. The new elite structure, which has emerged during the last half a century, shows changes in the following three directions : (i) number and influence of rural-based elites is increasing; (ii) members of the non-upper castes are also acquiring elite positions on a significant scale; and (iii) elites representing regional, ethnic and economic interests are increasing their power at state level (ibid: 1-7).

Altekar and Puri (1955) have given a full account of the political set up of the ancient village communities. "During the nineteenth century, under the general influence of the theory of social evolution, several social philosophers made a special study of the genesis and development of land tenure, inheritance of property, primitive and rural jurisprudence and other social institutions in the different parts of the world" (Vidyarthi, 1967: 12).

Maine (1871) and Powell (1896) have studied Indian villages for specific purposes, for comparative jurisprudence and for administration. These studies have a direct bearing on the political system and leadership pattern of the village communities, and are examples of the first attempts in this field of study.

Lewis (1954) and Dhillon (1955) have studied factions and leadership in north and south Indian villages. Their studies on the power structure in rural India inspired a number of other American, British and Indian scholars to take up the study of rural leadership in the villages of the different parts of India. Yogendra Singh (1955) had worked on the changing power structure in six villages in eastern UP and brings out the characteristics of traditional and emerging power structure in them.

Srinivas (1959) and Dube (1961) have studied the pattern of rural leadership. Srinivas regards the concept of dominant caste as crucial for understanding of power relations in rural social life. Dube finds that the political power is concentrated in a few individuals rather than diffused in the structure among the two Hinduized tribes, the Bhumij and the Bhil, and refers to the utility of the historical perspective in understanding the changing authoritarian structure of the two groups.

N.D. Kamble (1982), in his study on the scheduled caste parliamentarians and state legislators, observes that they depend on the higher caste leadership in order to be elected. They are always at the mercy of higher caste leaders to get share in the power for their selfish motives and to emerge superiors among the scheduled castes. Sangwan (1986) has studied the awareness and role performance of Harijan legislators of Haryana for the period 1977-79. He observed that they were discriminated politically and were never consulted by higher caste legislators while political decisions were taken. They never protested against such decisions and they were neglected mainly because of lack of unity among them. Sagwan's study refers to one time small period, that too of a very small number (17 legislators) and limited to a few aspects only. Nothing can be generalized based on such study.

Sachchidananda's (1977) study of *Harijan elites* is a path breaking study of social, administrative and political elites among the scheduled castes in Bihar. He identifies elites of three types through web approach and networks of the scheduled castes. Raj Bala (1997) studied scheduled caste leaders in Rohtak district of Haryana and observed that scheduled caste leaders had been playing a role of an emulsion among their caste people and extracting aids and grants from various governmental agencies for the community welfare activities.

Muni (1970) has also emphasized the same view. Hazel D' Lima (1983) studied women in local government in Maharashtra. In his study of women in Zilla Parishads it is observed that the women of upper castes, i.e. those belonging to the families of big landlords or politically influential try to dominate the positions reserved for women in the Zilla Parishads or Panchayat Samities.

Bhatt (1995) studied all 155 women members of Parliament (MPs) elected up to the sixth Lok Sabha (1977). She observed that most of them belonged to the middle class families. Women MPs from general constituencies had higher educational qualifications as compared to those elected from Reserved Constituencies.

Kumari and Dubey (1994) studied socio-economic conditions and other related issues like role of women MPs in Parliament proceedings, their association with political parties, the hindrance faced by them and their involvement in the electoral politics. They have covered all the women MPs of tenth Lok Sabha along with the women members of the Upper House; totalling 74. She found that many women MPs belonged to families having political background, with support of their parents or their spouses; they had established themselves in the party organizations. Although, they tried to raise various issues but most of them seemed to be more concerned with the issues related to women. Irrespective of their party's affiliation, the women MPs seemed to unite and took a common stand on the floor of the House on women specific issues. They also expressed their concerns about the indifference of the male parliamentarians. However, based on this study, no generalization or conclusion can/should be drawn as the sample covers only 24 women MPs, only one-third of the universe.

Kaushik (1993-1996) has studied women in politics in India. In her study, the sample of women politicians was drawn from national, regional and local levels, which covered ministers, MPs, legislators, members occupying important positions, members of District Boards, Local Village Bodies, common women. She distributed the sample totalling 80, under different headings: National = 56, State = 14 and Districts = 8. From the survey of 80 women politicians and 300 common women from different regions and classes, she found that majority of women politicians were drawn from middle class urban family background. Sixty-three per cent of middle class common women disapproved of their family members' participation in politics, as it was considered a "dirty", "corrupt" and "immoral" vocation (Kaushik, 1993: 53-81). Some other researchers have also arrived at similar findings.

The various studies done so far reveal that majority of the women, who are actively engaged in politics, have come from economically well off families and have at least one of her close relatives mostly father, husband or mother also involved in the active politics and shows linkage of their political career with their families. In many a cases, the facilitator of women politician's career has been a prominent leader who holds an important position in his party and in decision-making committees of the party. Even scheduled castes and scheduled tribes women leaders generally belonged to the higher educational category and to economically well off families. Therefore, "the association between higher social and economic status and higher rate of participation is clearly established" (Bhatt, 1995: 71).

Seth (1979) has studied social background of women MPs from 1951 to 1979 in his Ph.D. thesis entitled *Political Participation of Women*, which is admired by the social scientists and the study is considered to be a White Book on women MPs of Gujarat. He has observed that most of the women MPs belonged to economically well off families. Most of them were quite educated and some of them were very well educated. His astonishing revelation was that even the candidates from the scheduled castes or scheduled tribes generally belonged to the higher educational category. It was their background of higher education that gave them a perspective of politics and helped them in their understanding of public issues and political processes (Seth, 1979: 31).

Seth's (1979) study further pointed out that family background and a fairly high education harnessed during the work in social and public life made them articulate. This was largely in contrast with the glamorous MPs from the princely families. By their grooming and background the latter were neither painstaking nor much articulate. Most of them belonged to the Rightist parties like the Swatantra and the Jana Sangh. But those belonging to the Congress, and latter to the Janata Party in the 6th Lok Sabha, were the ones who made their presence felt in Parliament. The average age of the women candidates was 51.3 years and majority of the women MPs were married to people belonging to middle age group and higher middle-income group. None was illiterate and most of them were well educated. Income and education-wise they were better placed than the average male MPs. The largest group had their linkage with various social, cultural and women's organizations. Many of them had been active in freedom movement and, after independence, they entered active politics through Congress Party (Bhatt, 1995: 70).

The study also referred to the "male equivalence factor". This factor applies to a situation in which a woman seeks to gain in political position as a substitute for a man. Thus, it appears that in a "widow succession case", a woman candidate mostly succeeds a husband in his constituency on the death of her husband. This has been more marked in the cases of the person assuming the political role of an agitator or that of taking up the causes that her husband stood for than in the position of the power. This may also be considered as a function with political background families (ibid: 71).

"The association between higher social and economic status and higher rate of participation is also established. Only in the case of women activists with family linkages, this view may be slightly modified because linkage, irrespective of education, is a powerful factor in a woman's politicization in leading, may be to instrument in practical politics" (ibid: 71). There is one more factor that influences the politicization and participation of women in politics. The factor that shows the significance of the background of their political career is their family linkage. The interest and understanding acquired through father, husband, brother and such other relations constitute the familial influence for women activists. The incidence of membership of politicized family is much more obvious in the case of the candidates belonging to the Congress and Communist Parties. The women have emerged as leaders through contesting elections. Most of them demonstrated their survival capacity in politics by getting themselves elected twice or thrice and few of them even five times. Another factor found to be responsible for their selection as candidates is the personal charisma and impact they had made in the major cities or their constituencies (ibid: 71).

Women leaders are active members of their party and raised a number of women's issues and got them included into the party's manifesto, as a representative of their areas as well as those of general concern. In some studies it is found that women leaders in parliament raise a variety of issues some of which are women specific while many others are not. The issues vary from black money in India to disasters caused by natural calamities, management of food grains, problems of unemployment, etc. The constraints which women generally face in entering into active politics are given tradition, physiology, lack of vertical mobility, concerns for family and home and psychology.

One of the major and most common areas of research on women and politics in contemporary India is their political participation. The subject dealt with the sphere of formal electoral politics. Hence political participation is, by and large, interpreted as the voting behaviour of women voters. This is partly due to the dominant role which electoral politics plays in parliamentary democracy in India, and partly to the dominance of the behavioural approach in social sciences, in general (Kaushik, 1993: 63).

Even while women constitute 45 per cent of agricultural labour in India, and have been participating in the peasant movements since the Moplah rebellions to the Telengana and Tebhaga Movements, there is very little writing on women's participation in them. A few papers are now available in the form of seminar presentations which show that even while there was enough evidence of women's involvement both in general issues of class and specific issues of women combined with class issues (as in Tebhaga), these have not been sufficiently explored. The question has also been raised in one of these papers as to how far women had any role in decision-making and what the impact was of women's participation on their status in the family and movement (ibid: 53-81).

The research done on the industrial sector has been of a similar nature. However, it is more extensive in scale when compared to work on peasant struggles. Many articles in journals, papers read in seminars and conferences and reports constitute the bulk of this literature. These micro-level studies unfold developments, women's participation, their demands and methodology in each struggle. They also examine the follow up of their participation and its impact on women themselves, and generally conclude that this led to the strengthening of the women's movement as such. There are also several dissertations on the working women (Kaushik, 1993: 64).

A few books have been written on women in local government and politics, e.g. Nivedita Menon (1999), Sangeeta Purushothaman (1998), Bhavana Jharta (1996), Shusheela Kaushik (1993), Ranjana Kumari (1992), Sumana Pandey (1990), J.K. Baral (1990), etc. They deal with only a few regions of India. Of late, some papers published in seminars, Economic and Political Weekly, national dailies have also taken up the theme such as women reservation, the role of women in politics, extent and nature of their participation in the local government (known otherwise as Panchayati Raj), the statutory provisions, the nature of selection (nomination, co-option, direct and indirect elections etc.), the limitations and advantages therein. These aspects have been analyzed at length in various papers.

Though undertaken on a local and regional basis, covering the states of Andhra Pradesh, Karnataka, Madhya Pradesh, Punjab and Uttar Pradesh, these studies, by and large, arrive at the same conclusions. They have assumed a particular significance, in the past few years, with India attempting large-scale changes and reforms in its local government system. Women, along with other weaker sections, have begun to receive some attention (ibid: 64).

Kaushik (1993), in her study on women's role and participation in Panchayati Raj, has arrived at the following findings :

i. The participation of women is low in terms of number and quality. A majority (little more than 50 per cent) is over the age of 50. Most of them belong to the affluent land owning, high caste families and are related to politically active sections of the societies;
ii. Political awareness as well as participation and knowledge of wider issues are below the mark. The co-option of women is more a tokenism than real representation; and
iii. The continuation of nomination — co-option or even reservation — is a reflection of the continuing inability of women to get elected through the normal process (ibid: 66).

Because of the factors noted above, the role of the state level politicians has become distinct from those at the national level. As such the study of political elites at the state level and their perception of social, political and economic changes acquires greater importance. Keeping this in view, the study of political elites at the state level, particularly of the women legislators, is likely to be more fruitful and important.

The studies done so far merely confirm the popular impression that: (i) women are not independent voters; (ii) that a majority are illiterate; (iii) that a majority make their choice on the basis of suggestions from male members of the family — husbands and sons; (iv) that they lack information and political awareness; and (v) that they were not politically conscious (Kaushik, 1993: 53-81).

A deeper analysis of the socio-economic and cultural factors, more particularly the family position and the power relations within the family, and of factors that prevent the women from gaining access to political information and education are totally lacking. Equally conspicuous by its absence is the analysis of any mobilization and organization of women, their participation in activities/ organizations during the inter-election period. In the absence of such a participation and exposure to other than familial sources and activities, women cannot be expected to have developed an independent political consciousness.

The studies on women's political participation at the state level in panchayats, districts and particularly in legislatures are very rare. Also, detailed studies of women leaders in State Legislatures and Parliament, their roles and contributing factors for their emergence as leaders and their problems in entry to active politics have not been done exhaustively and such studies are few.

3

AREA OF STUDY
The Context

The study has been conducted in the state of Uttar Pradesh (UP). The research work, which began in 1996 as an academic exercise just after the elections of the Uttar Pardesh (UP) State Assembly, was completed in the year 2001. In this period of five years, three important events took place, which changed the whole data on the State's population, geographical area, political position with regards to the numbers of Members of Legislative Assembly (MLA) and Members of Parliament (MP) as well as many other socio-economic indicators without having much impact on the outcome of the study.

First event, state of UP was divided in two parts. A new state "Uttaranchal" was created in November 2000 carving out from UP bifurcating the hill region, comprising 13 districts covering an area of 53483 square kilometres and population of 84,79,562 as per the 2001 Census. This development has changed all key parameters of State. Efforts were made to revise and up-date the data, but some of the figures remained to be segregated for both the states, separately.

The second, State Government issued a new notification for caste classifications and some castes, which were in general category earlier were brought under a new class; the Other Backward Caste (OBC) in 2001 resulting in reservation policy for legislators in the assembly.

And the third important episode, which took place, was that the fourteenth assembly elections were declared and conducted in 2002 first time after bifurcation. It was thought appropriate to cover the fourteenth elections to make the study spanking new as earlier it was meant to cover the women legislators up to the thirteenth assembly and therefore, the whole text of the book was revised. However, it was observed that all these developments have no momentous impact on the findings except change in parameter's profile of state.

Some of the basic facts about U.P. after bifurcation are as under :

A. 1. Area in lakh sq. km. 2.41
2. Population in lakh (2001) 1661
3. Number of Districts 70
4. Number of Development Blocks 809
5. No. of Villages (Habitat) (1991) 97134

B. Comparative figures of UP and All-India

S.No.	*Particulars*	*U.P.*	*All-India*
1.	Per capita in Rs. at current price *(1999-2000)	9765	16047
2.	Growth of per capita income *1999-2000 at current price over the previous year (%)	7.6	9.1
3.	Population in lakh (2001)	1661	10270
4.	Percentage of urban population (2001)	20.76	27.78
5.	Decadal Growth rate during 1991-2001	25.80	21.34
6.	Density of population per sq. km. (2001)	689	324
.	Sex ratio (no. of females—per thousand males) (2001)	898	933
8.	Birth rate per thousand (2000)	32.8	25.8
9.	Death rate per thousand (2000)	10.3	8.5
10.	Infant mortality rate (2000)	83	68
11.	Population below poverty line in percentage* (1999-2000)		
	Rural	31.22	27.09
	Urban	30.89	23.62
12.	Literacy rate in percent (2001)	57.36	65.38
	Male	70.23	75.85
	Female	42.98	54.16
13.	Electrified villages in Nos. (up to March 2000)	89117	

* Figures pertains to undivided Uttar Pradesh

Source : Tenth Five Year Plan (2002-07) and Annual Plan (2002-03) Volume-I, Government of Uttar Pradesh (Part-I), State Planning Commission (April, 2002)

UP is politically a very sensitive and important state, more pronounced in providing leadership. The state of UP, which is socially more backward than many of the other states, has sent more women into the Centre and State legislatures than any other. It has the largest Legislative Assembly, sends largest number of MPs in the Parliament and always dominates the national scene.

The state has always been a deciding factor for the leadership at the Centre by virtue of its large representation of 80 in the parliament (15.70 per cent of the total strength). It also has the largest Legislative Assembly in the country by having 404 assembly seats. This factor is important for the election of the head of the country also. The state has given many men and women leaders of national and international repute to the country. In fact, the first man and the first woman Prime Ministers in India belonged to this state. The state had first woman Chief Minister, first woman Governor, first woman Secretary General to UN and many more firsts. It has given maximum number of Prime Ministers to the country. Out of thirteen Prime Ministers of India, Uttar Pradesh has given eight. Both formal and informal leadership can be observed in this state. That is why UP has been selected as the area of the present study.

The state provides a specific situation by its location, general reputation, large size of population, large women voters, social composition, socio-cultural history and an important centre of political activities. The demographic and other important salient features of UP, position of women in state, their political activities, organizations and political parties are described in subsequent paragraphs.

Uttar Pradesh with 70 districts, 300 tehsils, 809 development blocks, 97134 villages and an area of 2.41 Lakh sq. km is the fifth largest state of the country area-wise after Madhya Pradesh Rajasthan and Maharashtra (UP State Annual Plan, 2002-2003). The state covers 7.34 per cent of the total geographical area of the country while the percentage of share of the state in the total population of the country is 16.17. As a result, the availability of geographical area in the state is 1.45 sq km for every one thousand of population, which is 62.6 per cent less than the corresponding figure of 3.88 sq km for the country.

3.1 Demography : Pressure on Population

It has the highest share of 16.17 per cent in the country's total population. According to 2001 census, the total population of the state was 1661 lakh. As per the National Health Survey (NHS) 1999-2000, the population of UP has gone up to 1715 lakh and, thus, there is an increase of 23.3 per cent over the 1991-2000 period. The scheduled caste population is 21.05 per cent, which is much higher than 16.48 per cent at the national level and is the highest among all major states except Punjab (28.31 per cent) and West Bengal (23.62 per cent).

The percentage of rural and urban population in total population was 79.24 per cent (1316 lakhs) and 20.26 per cent (345 lakhs) respectively. In the decade 1981-91, the urban population increased by 38.7 per cent while it was 36.5 per cent at the national level. The share of urban population in the total population of the state has increased from 17.95 per cent in 1981 to 19.80 per cent in 1991 and 20.76 per cent in 2001 against the corresponding percentages of 23.31 and 27.78 respectively at the national level.

The sex ratio in Uttar Pradesh has declined from 910 in 1951 to 885 in 1981, further to 879 in 1991 and 898 in 2001. The corresponding figures at all India level were 946 in 1951, 934 in 1981 and 927 in the year 1991 and 933 in 2001. Among the states, sex ratio is the highest in Kerala (1036).

3.2 Working Force

The percentage increase in workers in the state was 31.56 during 1981-91 against an increase of 25.48 per cent in its total population during this period. The total number of workers increased from 340.52 lakh in 1981 to 448.00 lakh in 1991 and the proportion of workers to total state's population moved up from 30.7 to 32.2 per cent. The share of workers in state's population (32.2 per cent) is considerably lower than the corresponding figure of 37.1 per cent at national level. With 32.7 per cent workers in total population, the state ranked 9th among major states except Andhra Pradesh (45.0 per cent), Tamil Nadu (43.3 per cent), Maharashtra (43.0 per cent), Madhya Pradesh (42.8 per cent), Karnataka (42.0 per cent), Gujarat (40.2 per cent), Rajasthan (38.9 per cent) and Orissa (37.5 per cent). All these seven states (except Orissa) are ahead of UP in per capita income also. Punjab, Haryana and Kerala though have lower work participation ratio of 30.9 per cent, 31.0 per cent and 31.9 per cent per cent respectively, but have a higher per capita state income (UP Annual Plan, 2000-01:42-46).

The percentage share of total workers in rural population also increased from 31.5 to 33.5 during the decade 1981-91. Likewise, the share of female workers in female population moved up from 9.0 per cent to 14.2 per cent during the aforesaid decade while the share of male workers in total male population declined by 51.5 per cent to 50.5 per cent in 1981-91. The share of urban female workers in urban female population also moved up from 3.5 per cent to 4.8 per cent during the decade 1981-91, but the share of workers in urban population slipped down from 27.3 per cent to 27.1 per cent. In the same way, the share of male workers in total male population also declined from 47.5 per cent in 1981 to 46.4 per cent in 1991 (ibid : 42-46).

According to 1991 census, villages having population below 500 were 40.1 per cent of the total inhabited villages, which are characterized as small villages. The percentage of such villages in the state is higher than that of other developed states like Punjab (30.9 per cent), Maharashtra (29.0 per cent), Gujarat (21.6 per cent), Haryana (16.0 per cent) and Tamil Nadu (13.1 per cent). These villages in the state have a considerably higher share as 9.9 per cent of its total population greater than the percentage in Punjab (7.1 per cent), Maharashtra (6.8 per cent), Gujarat (4.2 per cent), Haryana (2.4 per cent) and Tamil Nadu (1.6 per cent) (ibid : 42-46).

3.3 Economy of the State of UP

In 1980-81, the total state income at current prices was Rs. 14012 crore, which increased to Rs. 21514 crore in 1984-85, Rs. 41664 crore in 1989-90, Rs. 57206 crore in 1991-92, Rs. 88511 crore in 1995-96 and further to Rs. 113105 crore in 1997-98, registering an increase of 53.5 per cent during 1981-85, 93.7 per cent in 1985-90, 37.3 per cent during 1990-92, 54.7 per cent during 1992-96 and 27.8 per cent during 1996-98 (ibid : 42-46). In spite of these increases, the state's contribution to total national income declined from 12.7 per cent to 11.6 per cent in 1980-81 and 1984-85 respectively. It slightly increased to 11.7 per cent in 1989-90 and 11.9 per cent in 1991-92, but again slipped down to 10.2 per cent in 1996-97.

The per capita income of the state has been lower than the per capita income of the country. The per capita state income, at current prices, increased from Rs. 1278 in 1980-81 to Rs. 1784 in 1984-85, Rs. 3087 in 1989-90, Rs. 4069 in 1991-92, Rs. 5872 in 1995-96 and Rs. 9765 in 2000. But the gap between the per capita state income and the per capita national income also widened (ibid : 42-46).

In order to improve the well being of women and children in society the government has made a significant shift in the approach from 'welfare during fifties' to 'development' during seventies and to 'empowerment' during the nineties. During the nineties major thrust in respect of women was to ensure them economic independence and self-reliance, while in respect of children, efforts were made to ensure their 'survival, protection and development' with special focus on the girl child and adolescent girl (ibid: 42-46).

Constitution of India also gives support and strength to them as its Article 14 confers equal rights and opportunities for men and women in the political, economic and social spheres; Article 15 prohibits discrimination against any citizen on the ground of sex, religion, race and caste, etc.; Article 16 provides for equality of opportunities in the matter of public appointments for all citizens; Article 39 mentions that the State shall direct its policy towards providing to men and women equally the right to means of livelihood, human conditions of work and maternity relief whereas Article 51(A)(e) imposes a fundamental duty on every citizen to renounce the practices derogatory to the dignity of women.

3.4 Literacy

Female literacy rose from 0.69 per cent in 1901 to 18.4 in 1971 in India, but because of the tremendous increase in population, this improvement has not been able to offset the overall increase in the number of illiterate women.

Census data indicate that during the past 20 years (1971-91) male and female literacy in UP has increased by 24-23 and 14.76 percentage points respectively. As compared to census data, the results of 53rd round of National Sample Survey indicate that during the past 6 years (1991-97) the state has achieved a remarkable progress. During this period, the increase in male and female literacy rate is 8.87 and 10.81 percentage points respectively at all India level whereas the corresponding figures are 13.27 and 15.69 percentage points at the UP state level.

Census 1991 data also reveals the highest discrimination in male-female literacy in BIMARU (Bihar, Madhya Pradesh, Rajasthan, Uttar Pradesh) states. This discrimination is nearly 34 percentage points in Rajasthan as compared to 30 percentage points each in UP, Madhya Pradesh and Bihar. The state of UP has low female literacy 42.98 per cent than all India average (54.16%).

3.5 Political History of UP in General

In ancient times, UP was known as Madhya Desh. The entire region extending up to Prayag in the east bore the name of Madhya Desh. It was considered sacred in Hindu mythology as gods and heroes mentioned in the two epics — *Ramayana* and *Mahabharata*—lived here. Its subsequent history got mingled with the *Puranas* and other Hindu scriptures. From sixth century BC, the history of this region can be properly recovered. During Hindu period, the state has seen rise and fall of several dynasties such as the Kurus and Panchalas, Kosala and Kashi, Kushans and the Gupta dynasty. After the fall of the Gupta dynasty in the 6th century AD, this region was ruled by regional dynasties—the Mukharies of Kannauj and Harshwardhan of Thaneshwar. The Gurjar Pratiharas and Gaharwaras held their sway over the Gangetic plains during 9th and 10th centuries. The history of Madhya Desh in 13th and 14th centuries is a saga of brave resistance and barbaric repression.

The Sultans, the Mughals and the Nawabs of Awadh ruled over this area. By the middle of the eighteenth century, the Nawabs of Awadh had come in contact with the East India Company (EICo). In 1784 AD, Mir Kasim was forced to cede the districts of Kara and Allahabad to the Company. The territories obtained from the

Nawabs during 1775-1801 were initially attached to the Bengal Presidency and were known as Conquered and Ceded Provinces. The EICo under the treaty of Sanguli took the Kumaon and Garhwal regions in 1816 (Rana, 2000 : 354).

As a result of expansion of the territories of the East India Company (EICo) beyond Oudh, a new administrative unit under the Lieutenant Governor, called the North-Western Province (NWP), was created in 1836 AD. Agra was placed under a Chief Commissioner. In 1858, the Delhi Division was taken out from the NWP and its capital shifted from Agra to Allahabad. In November of the same year the political power was transferred from the EICo to the British Crown (ibid: 354).

Later in 1877, Oudh territories were combined with it and it was renamed as the North-Western Provinces of Agra & Oudh. Its name was again changed in 1902 AD to United Provinces of Agra and Oudh. It was made a Governor's Province in 1921 and its capital shifted to Lucknow. In 1937, the words Agra and Oudh were dropped and it was named as United Province. After Independence, the native States of Tehri Garhwal, Rampur and Banaras were merged with it and in 1950 it was renamed Uttar Pradesh (ibid: 354).

The state has a bicameral legislature. The State Assembly consists of 404 members. The Legislative Council has 100 Members; ninety-two seats are reserved for the SCs and one for the STs in the Assembly. It sends 31 members to the Rajya Sabha.

3.6 Elections in UP — Some Aspects

Politics of the state of UP since its formation in 1950 has been, until the 1967 elections, the politics of the Congress party. In fact, ever since the achievement of independence in 1947, the state was placed under the government of the Congress party. The Congress leadership in the state, very appropriately, built up a strong base for itself among the rural masses of the state by introducing some fundamental land reforms giving the peasantry proprietary rights over the land they tilted or complete security of tenure. A number of schemes were launched for the uplift of the countryside. They were also given a feeling of participation in the management of some local matters through the Panchayati Raj system. All these measures carried the Congress in power through the years. There was only a weak opposition in the State Legislature.

But during the second half of the twenty-year period since Independence, the opposition began to grow more significantly. The ruling party steadily lost its popularity on account of a number of factors. In the elections of 1952, the opposition and independent candidates together secured a little over 52 per cent of the total votes polled. In ten years' time in the elections of 1962, this percentage rose to 63 per cent (Varma & Narain, 1968: 371).

Of the opposition parties, before the fourth general elections, the Jana Sangh had a steady growth. It had emerged as the largest opposition group in the State Assembly after the elections of 1962. It had nearly fifty members in a house of 430. The socialist parties also had a good position in the Assembly but they failed to combine and constitute a single group or party in the legislature, which could have been larger than the Jana Sangh. It must also be mentioned that up to 1966, there has been no Muslim communal group of any importance in the politics of the state (Varma & Narain, 1968: 372).

Except for a brief period, when Bhartiya Kranti Dal (BKD) formed the government under the Chief Ministership of Chaudhary Charan Singh, the Congress Party was comfortably placed in the Assembly till 1977. In 1977, the Janata Party replaced the Congress as the majority party. Ram Naresh Yadav of the Janata party became the Chief Minister. The Janata Government did not complete its full term and the Congress Party came into power in the middle of the year 1980. Later, in the Assembly elections to Uttar Pradesh, the Congress Party was badly defeated and Mulayam Singh Yadav, a non-Congressman, became the Chief Minister whose term lasted between December 1989 to June 1991. In the Assembly elections of 1991, the BJP formed the Government headed by Kalyan Singh. His government was dismissed in the wake of demolition of *Babri Masjid's* disputed structure on December 6, 1992, after having a term of just less than two years. In 1993, Assembly elections were held in UP, thereafter Mulayam Singh Yadav of the Samajwadi Party, supported by the BSP, which also became a partner in the

Govenunent, again became the Chief Minister (Aggarwal and Chowdhry, 1996:171).

In the Assembly polls of 1993, all non-BJP parties united to defeat the BJP, but despite this 'unity' BJP remained the single largest party by winning 176 seats with 33.36 per cent votes. The SP-BSP alliance had won only 168 seats but it formed a government, which was, headed by Mulayam Singh Yadav and lasted for one and a half years. Then due to the differences with the SP, the BSP Secretary General Ms. Mayawati formed a new government that remained in power for 135 days (ibid: 173).

The UP Assembly was dissolved on October 27, 1995. The 1996 elections demonstrated the sliding influence of the JD and the Left Parties in UP. The JD, already weakened by successive splits, was given a severe blow by Mulayam Singh Yadav, whose Government the JD had supported unconditionally.

The last few elections in UP had demonstrated that the Congress, the JD and Left parties are becoming politically irrelevant in the largest populated state of the country. Only the SP and BSP fighting each other issuing rank casteist appeal and inducing Muslims would face the BJP. The BSP, however, vastly improved upon its earlier performance of 1991. The gain of 69 Assembly seats in the 1993 elections in alliance with the Samajwadi Party was an exception. After parting ways with the SP, the BSP has not lost its clout and has demonstrated that it is emerging as a force to reckon with and has the Dalit votes are solidly behind it, plus a chunk of lower caste Muslims and OBCs.

The most significant aspect is the substantial increase in the poll percentage of the BSP, which touched about 18 per cent against nearly 19 of the SP. It is true that the SP contested only 64 seats against 85 by the BSP in UP, however, the accretion of the BSP vote compared to that of the SP is significant. The BJP vote percentage, which had showed an increase up to 34 per cent in the 1993 Assembly elections, came down to 31 per cent (Aggarwal & Chowdhry, 1996:173).

In 1993 elections the Samajwadi Party and the Bahujan Samaj Party joined hands, and the BJP was handed a crushing defeat. The tactical understanding ended within two years and the SP leader

Mr. Mulayam Singh Yadav, and the BSP leader Ms. Mayawati, fell apart since then. In successive elections since 1993, Mr. Mulayam Singh had been adopting a pro-Left stance. He even helped members of the Communist parties got elected to the Assembly. During this phase, the Congress had a direct understanding with the BSP. The SP has developed a strong dislike for both the BSP and the Congress. Mr. Mulayam Singh's refusal to extend support to Mrs. Sonia Gandhi after the fall of the Vajpayee Government only worsened the situation. The two Left parties, which were to be electoral allies of Mr. Yadav, have also drifted away (Rana, 2000: 355).

3.7 Electoral Scene 1999

The latest Lok Sabha election was held in 1999. It would be worth looking at a glance through the electoral scene of 1999. The non-BJP parties in the state had all claimed that they were fighting the LS polls to strengthen secularism, but they were as disunited as possible. They failed to arrive at a tactical understanding to extend indirect help to each other — *vis-a-vis* their sworn enemy — the BJP. In their mutual acrimony, they did not mind that the nature of contest became favourable to the BJP, which was opposed by all of them.

3.7.1 *The Muslims*

The Muslims hold a key to power in the state. They comprise about 17 per cent of the votes and as such are one of the major vote blocks in the state. They can tilt the scale in at least 20 of the 85 Lok Sabha constituencies and can influence voting pattern in other constituencies as well. The INC looked to them for its revival and the BSP for its survival (Rana, 2000:355).

Despite their numerical strength in as many as 20 constituencies, only eight Muslims managed to get elected to LS this time. Of the lucky eight, three were from the BSP, two each from the INC and SP and one from RLD. The BSP had fielded the highest number of 17 Muslim debutants, SP 15, INC 11, RLD two and the BJP one (ibid: 356).

3.7.2 *Dalit-Muslim Votes*

If keeping the BJP out of power was the sole consideration of Muslims in Uttar Pradesh then they had every reason to vote en bloc for the BSP. It was the BSP that sealed the fate of the BJP-led Government at the crucial vote of confidence in 1999 (ibid : 356). Dalits and Muslims together roughly constitute 39 per cent of the electorate in the state (Dalits 21.6 per cent and Muslims 17 per cent). This is 4 per cent higher than the BJP's 36.49 per cent vote share in the 1998 polls. The DM formula can work wonders in the state and unsettle the existing political scenario. There are 71 Lok Sabha constituencies in the state where Muslims and Dalits together constitute more than 30 per cent of the electorate. In 57 constituencies, they constitute 35 per cent and above. In fact, there are 37 such seats where the Dalit-Muslim combination constitute 40 per cent and above of the total electorate (ibid: 357). Thus, it may be concluded that Dalit-Muslim combination in the UP elections may play very important role in deciding political structure in the state and to some extent in the Centre as well.

4

WOMEN LEGISLATORS IN UTTAR PRADESH
An Overview

4.1 Women and Political Parties — General Observations

In a democratic set up, the political road to decision making usually leads to the system via the political parties. Thus while analyzing the role and participation of women members in various political parties, it becomes imperative to see, in general, the promises or programmes they have for the upliftment of women in their manifestoes, and to what extent they encourage women within their party organizations. What is the scope of actual role and participation for women members in each party? In the following discussion, an attempt has been made to study the background of various political parties *vis-a-vis* their plans to solve the women's issues.

The Congress is one of the oldest parties in India. It was founded in 1885 at the initiative of Mr. A.O. Hume. Its main objective was the well-being and the advancement of the people and the establishment of free India by peaceful and legitimate means of a cooperative commonwealth based on equality of opportunity and of political, economic and social rights aiming at world peace and fellowship (Kumari, 1994: 61).

Looking at Congress Party's attitude towards women, it was observed that after Independence, efforts have been made for the upliftment and empowerment of women. It gave a legal shape to many Acts for the upliftment of women, such as Hindu Marriage Act (1955), Maternity Benefit Act (1961), the Child Marriage Act (1976), Dowry Prohibition Act (1961), the Equal Remuneration Act (1976), the Suppression of Immoral Traffic in Women and Girls Act (1856), Indecent Representation of Women Prohibition

Act (1956), the Commission of Sati Act (1987), etc. In 1984, the party decided to constitute a Mahila Congress at its session held at Bangalore. A draft Constitution was framed at the Convention. It was decided to set up units of the Mahila Congress from the block to the AICC level. At present it has three state level units.

With its headquarters at Jawaharlal Bhawan in New Delhi, the Mahila Congress (Women's Wing of the Indian National Congress) has an 11-point Action Plan which includes working for communal harmony, health and hygiene, campaign against drug addiction, green belt programme, widow and old age pension, legal aid to the needy and also to educate women regarding their rights.

Objective of the Mahila Congress, according to Kumudben Joshi, is to ensure women's participation in public life, end of discrimination again them, improve the conditions of working women and end superstitions to promote a scientific temper (ibid: 62).

Even a cursory look at their manifesto indicates that it has special programmes and promises for the empowerment of women. It promises to implement Indira Mahila Yojana and National Perspective Plan for women. It also promises 30 per cent membership in local government and other statutory bodies and also promise that committees will be reserved for women.

In the year 1977, the Janata Government emerged as a powerful alternative to Congress Party. It was formed with the merger of four political parties — the Congress (O), the Socialist Party, the Jan Sangh and the Bharatiya Lok Dal. Later, Congress for Democracy merged with the Janata Party. Basically, this party was formed as an alliance of those groups, whose common interest were to fight against the authoritarian rule of the Congress headed by Mrs. Indira Gandhi. Ideologically, the five components of the Janata Party did not have much in common. Before the Janata Party was formed, they were advocating different viewpoints. The Congress (O), that came into existence after the split of the Indian National Congress in 1969, had no unique act of economic programmes. The party, in its election manifesto for the Fifth General Election, had affirmed its faith in a truly Democratic and Socialist Society.

The Socialist Party, which had a history of splits and mergers, had emerged as a United Socialist Party in 1971 after the Samyukt

Socialist Party (SSP), the Praja Socialist Party (PSP) and Indian Socialist Party decided to form a new party. The programme of the PSP consisted of moderate socialist nature, which advocated uplifting of India's economy through the use of Gandhian programme of small scale and cottage industries within the villages to achieve self-sufficiency. The SSP, on the other hand, proclaimed itself to be the party of revolutionary struggle. It expressed its lack of faith in automatic development of socialism and hence demanded radical economic changes.

When the PSP and SSP merged to form the Socialist Party, the goals of the newly formed party were described as achieving a socialist society free from social, political and economic exploitation of man by man and of nation by nation. It affirmed its faith in democratic and peaceful means to eliminate all forms of injustice and feudal capitalistic exploitation. It also favoured peaceful revolutionary class struggle.

The Janata Party made an attempt to emphasize its basic difference from its main political rival, the Congress Party. It projected itself as a party dedicated to the task of building up a democratic socialist State on the Gandhian principles drawing inspiration from our rich heritage and noble tradition of our struggle for national polity that ensures decentralization of economic and political power.

Distinct as it is from the other mainstream parties, the Bharatiya Janata Party (BJP) has a unique philosophy for its Mahila Morcha (the women's wing of Bharatiya Janata Party — a national level right wing political party in India), as well. Thus, while the left and left-leaning parties seek to liberate women, the BJP wants "puranee neev, naya nirman", which means new development but with roots in tradition (ibid: 63). According to the General Secretary of Morcha, "We don't want to turn women into men in the pursuit of equality. We want women's development, their progress, not fictional liberation. The womanhood of women must be protected at all costs first." Morcha organizes family counselling units at the state level to deal with problems that come to them for resolution. The Gujarat unit alone handled over 4,000 cases in the year 1993 (ibid: 63).

The BJP looks upon women-kind as "Matri-Shakti". In their various election manifestoes, they promised several steps for the improvement of socio-economic status of women, i.e. making women equal share holders in the husband's wealth and income, to strengthen family courts presided over by women judges to try all family related cases, get women equal pay for equal work, start more and more hostels for single woman, and suggest suitable remedial measures.

For the Janata Dal and Samajwadi Janata Party, the two other national parties, women have never been a top priority. Although women have separate units, they are mere appendages of the main party. According to a senior member, they are meant to be seen and heard. Women are like achar (pickles) but not essential, according to her (ibid: 64).

The Bharatiya Lok Dal was formed in 1974 when seven parties merged to form a new party. These parties were Swatantra, the Bharatiya Kranti Dal, the Utkal Congress, the SSP, the Bharatiya Khatikar Sangh, the Harijan Sangharsh Samiti and the Lok Tantrik Dal. The BKD was a party identified with the interests of the middle class, especially the middle-income farmers.

The Swatantra Party was committed to the system of free enterprise. The party vehemently criticized any encroachment on the freedom of the individual. The function of the State, according to the leaders of the Swatantra Party, is primarily to provide infrastructure on which private enterprise and initiative can enact the super structure.

National Front emerged as a alliance of five parties — the Janata Dal, Telugu Desam, Assam Gana Parishad, Congress (S) and DMK. "The National Front was committed to upholding the nation's honour and ushering a new social and economic order based on equality and justice. Talking about the women's issues, it said that our success in the national reconstruction would depend on the equal participation and involvement of women. The Front would, accordingly, give special attention to ensure this (ibid: 65).

According to the party's manifesto, "the basis for the social policy of the National Front shall be to guarantee women equality with men before law and to discourage and eliminate all those practices which militate against social equality of the sexes." It would make India a signatory to the UN Convention on Women's Rights and ensure that its policies and programmes for women flow from its charter.

The Janata Dal emerged as a new party in October 1998, which called for courageous and cohesive efforts to confront the vested interests and to bring about basic structural changes. According to Article 11 of the Janata Dal, the party is dedicated to building up a Democratic, Secular and Socialist State of India on the Gandhian principles, drawing inspiration from our rich heritage and the noble traditions of our struggle for national independence and individual liberty. The party believes in a policy that ensures decentralization of economic and political power. It affirms the right of peaceful and democratic dissent, which includes *satyagraha* or non-violent resistance.

Talking about the women's issues in the manifesto, the party advocated for the constitution of the National Commission for Women to ensure equal rights to them and to look into issues related to them. It also advocated that all legislations that discriminate against women and all laws concerning marriage, divorce, maintenance, custody, adoption and inheritance should be reviewed and special training in the agrarian sector, homes for the shelterless and social security should be extended to destitute women. Thirty per cent reservation for women in elections to Panchayati Raj and Municipal bodies, as provided in the Panchayati Raj and Nagar Palika Bill, shall be ensured. There should be a larger representation of women in the legislature.

Left parties in India emerged with the purpose of fighting for the exploitation of men by men, which is the key feature of a capitalist society. Transforming a society from capitalist to socialist is the only solution to this, according to the Leftist ideology.

In order to enhance women's participation in the party, Left parties realized need for their involvement. In the year 1954, the Left parties took up the task of women's issues through the women's forum that they had formed. The attitude of Left Parties towards the women's question is succinctly put by S.N. Tawale, "Theoretically, the approach of the Left Party towards the problem of emancipation of women is clear cut. According to it, the male-dominated social structure is an integral nature of the capitalist society. The exploitation of women by men and the men by the owners of the property are two links in the same chain. Any effort towards liberalization of women, therefore, is not likely to succeed without transforming the economic basis of society" (ibid: 65). In their manifestoes in 1991, they talked about the implementation of legal and democratic rights guaranteed in the Constitution, stop discrimination in pay scales, recruitment and promotions, proper working conditions for all working women, equal rights in land for them, etc.

Looking at ideologies and manifestoes of various political parties, one can perhaps conclude that majority of the parties are conscious of women related problems as a result they have women's wings in their parties and have specific promises or programmes for the enhancement of their status in general.

But to what extent they actually encourage women within their party organization can only be measured by the role women members play in the party organization, the extent to which women candidates have a say in the selection of candidates within their parties or their role in the entire decision-making process. To understand this, it is also important to understand the recruitment process or the criteria of selection followed in various parties. Whether it is the age, the occupational background, the profession or what is their political career or connections is to be carefully looked into.

4.2 National Scene

In the 1999 Lok Sabha elections, out of total 543 seats, 49 were gone to women. Thus, their representation in Indian Parliament is only 9 per cent. If we look at the statewise position, UP has the highest number of women MPs in the Lok Sabha. Out of total 85 seats in UP, 9 are women MP showing 10.58 per cent representation that is higher than the national average. The party-wise position of women parliamentarian shows that BJP has the highest women MPs. The statewise party position of women in 1999 election has been given in table 4.1 below.

Table 4.1 : State-wise Party Position of Women in 1999 Lok Sabha Elections in India

States	*INC*	*BJP*	*CP/M*	*NCP*	*RJD*	*AITC*	*TDP*	*BJD*	*SP*	*JD (S)/ INDP/Others*	*Total*
Andhra	1						4				5
Assam	1	1									2
Bihar	1				2						3
Chhatishgarh											
Gujarat		2									2
Haryana		1								1	2
Jharkhand		2									2
Karnataka	1										1
Kerala			1								1
MP		3									3
Maharashtra	1	1		1						1	4
Orissa	1	1						1			3
Punjab	2										2
Rajasthan	2	2								1	5
Tamil Nadu										1	1
UP	3	1							2	1	7
Uttaranchal											
W. Bengal			2			2					4
NCT		1									1
Total	13	15	3	1	2	2	4	1	2	5	48

Source: http://parliamentofindia.nic.in/

It can be seen from the above table that UP has the highest women representatives in the Lok Sabha at present. Similar trend was observed in the past. Congress had higher women representation in the earlier elections than other parties in the parliament, but in the present parliament, BJP has highest women representation as can be seen from the table. The women's representation in the state is another indicator. Party-wise women's representation in UP Assembly is given in the following table.

Table 4.2 : Party-wise Women Position in UP Assembly (1952-2002)

Sl. No.	*Year*	*Assembly*	*Total MLAs*	*No. of Women*	*%*	*BJP*	*INC*	*PSP/IND*	*SSP*	*BKD*	*JP*	*BSP*	*SP*	*RLD*
1	1952	Ist	347	11	3.17		11							
2	1957	IInd	341	24	7.0		23	1						
3	1962	IIIrd	430	20	4.65	1*	19							
4	1967	IVth	425	7	1.64		6		1					
5	1969	Vth	425	19	4.23		15		1	3				
6	1974	VIth	425	22	5.17		20			1	1			
7	1977	VIIth	425	12	2.82		4				8			
8	1980	VIIIth	425	20	4.70		17			2	1			
9	1985	IXth	425	31	7.30		26			5				
10	1989	Xth	425	19	4.47	2	8	1			7	1		
11	1991	XIth	425	10	2.35	6	1				3			
12	1993	XIIth	425	13	3.05	7						1	5	
13	1996	XIIIth	425	21	4.90	11		1				3	6	
14	2002	XIVth	404	26	6.4	6	1					6	12	1
15	Total	14	5772	255	4.44	33	151	3	2	11	20	11	23	1

Source: Prepared from the Data given in Election Commission's Reports (1952-2002)

It may be observed from the above table that Congress has the highest women representation till the tenth Assembly elections. In fact, after tenth elections, Congress' over-all position in UP Assembly has been declining continuously. In 1993 and 1996 elections, Congress could manage to win only 29 and 33 seats out of 424. This is one of the reasons that women in last three elections are not visible in the Congress.

4.3 Women Representation in UP Assembly before 1952

The UP Legislative Assembly was legally established in 1937, but prior to that the legislative council was very much in the existence since 1887. The participation of women in the legislative council was quite visible from the fact that Begum Azaz Rasul, popularly known as Kudesia Begum was elected unopposed as Deputy

Chairperson of the legislative council on 31st July 1937. At that time she was only 28 years old. She continued to be Dy. Chairperson till 1939.

4.4 Position of Women in UP Legislative Council

Although the main focus of the present study has been on the women in the Legislative Assembly, who were elected through electoral process after the independence, but women's position in the Legislative Council has also been cursorily examined. This may be worth looking in the Legislative Council in the preindependence era when Assembly was not constituted to judge women's position. Therefore, the root of women political participation in UP can be traced to pre-independence era when the first woman Smt. Saloni Ahemed and thereafter Smt. Lady Kailash Shrivastava were elected as members to the Legislative Council in the year 1933. The other woman who were elected as members to the Council in pre-independence era are given in Appendix-5. Their number was 5 only. Similarly, only nine (3.94%) women members were elected in the year 1942 and their names have been given in Appendix-5.1.

According to the Government of India Act, 1935, the 228 members in Legislative Council of UP had to be elected from 16 types of areas/regions/constituencies. There were six seats reserved for women, out of these six, one for general urban woman, three for general rural women and one each for Muslim urban and Muslim rural women. In 1937, 12 women members (5.26%) were elected to the Council. The names of women elected to the UP Legislative Council in 1937 is given in Appendix 5.

After implementation of the Constitution of India, from 5th May 1952 to 7th July 1982, only 36 women were elected to the Legislative Council of U.P. The total number of members elected to the Legislative Council during this period was 457. Therefore, the representation of women during 1952 to 1982 has been only 7.8 per cent. The list of women members elected to Legislative Council during this period is given in Appendix-5.

According to 1992 figures, the latest position of women members in Legislative Council is given in Appendix-5. Out of 110 members, the women members were only 7 and their representation during this period has been 6.3 per cent.

Though the visibility of women in Legislative Council of UP has been quite apparent since pre-independence era, but their representation has been very low. In fact, it has been only 5.26 per cent in 1937, 3.94 per cent in 1942 and 3.20 per cent in 1946.

4.5 The Women Representation in the Assembly after Independence

After independence, first Assembly elections were held in UP in the year 1952 wherein 11 women were elected. The total number of seats were 347. The percentage of the women legislators thus was only 3.16 per cent, which was quite low. However, the number of women legislators in the Assembly had increased in 1957 to 24 from 11 in 1952. In the year 1957, the total seats were 341 and the representation of women was 7.00 per cent. There have been fourteen elections in UP since 1952 and the last election was held in the year 2002. The representation of women in UP Assembly, more or less has been hovering around 4.00 to 4.50 per cent except two elections in the year 1967 and 1991 wherein their representation came down to 1.64 per cent and 2.35 per cent respectively. The other exceptional election was in the year 1985 wherein women had the highest representation, i.e.7.30 per cent. This has been due to the fact that the Congress had initiated policy to encourage women participation in politics and, therefore, women were preferred over men candidates while finalizing the nominations for elections. In fact, out of 31 women elected to the Assembly in 1985, 26 were from the Congress. The election-wise and year-wise position of women in UP Assembly has been shown in Table 4.3.

There are some inconsistencies in the figures given in the Report of the Election Commission and figures provided by the Assembly Secretariat. The difference in the figures may be because of the Election Commission reports contain the names of all the contestants who have been declared elected in a particular election. However, one may have resigned soon after her/his election and this would not be appearing in the list provided by the Assembly secretariat as it keeps records of sitting legislators.

The detailed name-wise, partywise and year-wise lists of the

Table 4.3 : Party-wise Position of Women Legislators in UP Assembly

Sl. No.	*Year*	*Assembly*	*No. of women*	*%*	*BJP*	*INC*	*PSP/ IND*	*SSP*	*BKD*	*JP*	*BSP*	*SP*	*RLD*
1	1952	First	11	3.17		11							
2	1957	Second	24	7.00		23	1						
3	1962	Third	20	4.65	1*	19		1					
4	1967	Fourth	7	1.64		6							
5	1969	Fifth	19	4.23		15		1	3				
6	1974	Sixth	22	5.17		20			1				
7	1977	Seventh	12	2.82		4				8			
8	1980	Eighth	20	4.70		17			2	1			
9	1985	Ninth	31	7.30		26			5				
10	1989	Tenth	19	4.47	2	8	1			7	1		
11	1991	Eleventh	10	2.35	6	1				3			
12	1993	Twelfth	13	3.05	7						1	5	
13	1996	Thirteenth	21	4.90	11		1				3	6	
14	2002	Fourteenth	26	5.94	6	1					6	12	1
15	Total	14	Total = 255	Avg. 4.44	33	151	3	2	11	20	11	23	1

Source: *Who's Who*, published by Secretariat of UP Assembly and Election Commission's Reports.

candidates are placed at Appendices-1to 8. It may be observed from the table above that Congress was leading till the last election giving more representation to the women. Actually, in the 1996 and 1993 elections, Congress' overall position was too bad and party lost many seats. That is one of the reasons that women in Congress party in last two elections were not visible in the UP Assembly. The position in each Assembly by their caste has been given in Table 4.4.

The representation of the women from SCs is sufficiently visible in the UP Assembly. In some of the elections, SCs have exceeded their prescribed numbers as per the reservation quota. There was no ST woman legislator in the UP Assembly.

The representation of the minorities, particularly that of the Muslim women, has been very thin. There were only three women legislators in the early years that have been consecutively elected to the Assembly. And in the later part, after 8th Vidhan Sabha, their representation has been almost non-existent. This may be due to the lower education rate among Muslim women and their less

Table 4.4 : Position of Women Legislators belonging to SCs & Minority Communities in UP Assembly

Sl. No.	*Year*	*Assembly*	*No. of Women*	*No. of SCs*	*%age*	*No. of Women From Minority*	*%age*
1	1952	First	11	2	18.18	0	00.00
2	1957	Second	24	7	29.16	0	00.00
3	1962	Third	20	6	30.00	0	00.00
4	1967	Fourth	7	3	42.80	0	00.00
5	1969	Fifth	19	3	15.70	2	10.52
6	1974	Sixth	22	8	23.80	1	4.76
7	1977	Seventh	12	3	25.00	1	8.33
8	1980	Eighth	20	3	15.00	1	5.00
9	1985	Ninth	31	7	22.58	2	6.45
10	1989	Tenth	19	4	21.05	0	00.00
11	1991	Eleventh	10	2	20.00	0	00.00
12	1993	Twelfth	13	5	38.46	0	00.00
13	1996	Thirteenth	21	9	42.85	0	00.00
14	2002	Fourteenth	26	14	53.84	2	7.70
			Total 255	76	Avg. 28.45	9	3.05

Source: Prepared from the Data given in Election Commission's Reports (1952-2002), Government of India.

personal liberty than their counterparts across the other communities.

There were fifty-six women who have represented their constituencies many times continuously. The list of those elected more than once and more is placed at Appendix-3.

4.6 Representation of Women in Ministerial Berths

The list of women legislators who have been Cabinet Ministers, State Ministers and Deputy Ministers in different council of ministers is placed at Appendix-4.

The representation of women in the ministerial births had been very low. In the first Assembly, there was not a single woman in the cabinet. In the second Assembly in 1957, Smt. Perkashwati Sood was the only Deputy Minister in the cabinet of Dr. Sampurnanand. When Shri Chander Bhan Gupta became the Chief

Minister, another woman Smt. Sucheta Kriplani was inducted in the cabinet as minister and Smt. Perkashwati Sood as Deputy Minister.

In the fourth Assembly, women representation in ministerial birth was zero. Till the eighth election only 2-3 women were made ministers in different cabinets and this trend has been consistent since fourth Assembly till the thirteenth elections. The exceptions have been the cabinets of Shri N.D.Tiwari and Shri Vir Bahadur Singh wherein women were given sufficient representation in ministerial berths in comparison to other Chief Ministers. The number of women ministers in their cabinets were 7 and 6 respectively. The total women elected in 1985 elections were 31 and out of them, 7 were made ministers representing 22 per cent. The detailed year-wise and cabinet-wise list of women ministers may be seen in Appendix-4.

It is quite visible that only few women were repeatedly given chances to become ministers. Therefore, in totality, women representation in ministerial berth has been really very low. It is also evident from the data that their representation continued to be low even when the state was headed by the women Chief Ministers, namely, Smt. Sucheta Kriplani in the third Assembly and Ms. Mayawati in 12th, 13th and 14th Assembly. Women representation in the ministerial berth plummeted further. Only one woman, Smt. Tara Aggarwal was minister in the cabinet of Smt. Sucheta Kriplani and Smt. Sushila was the only other woman minister in Ms. Mayawati's cabinet in the12th, 13th and 18th Assemblies. It was expected that the representation of women in ministerial berth would increase in the cabinet headed by the woman Chief Minister but this was rather reversed. This trend indicates that junior women legislators did not receive any support and co-operation nor any encouragement from their senior women legislators in the politics.

5

BACKGROUND, EMERGENCE AND ROLE OF WOMEN LEGISLATORS

In order to have in-depth appreciation of the elected representatives in a political system, it may be interesting to know their socio-economic status. The present chapter is an attempt to comprehend the socio-economic characteristics of the women legislators of Uttar Pradesh Legislative Assembly and to corelate such characteristics with the questions raised in the study regarding their background, emergence as leader, their role as politicians and their participation in the Assembly proceedings, etc.

For collection of data upon the above aspects a questionnaire was sent to all 95 present and past women legislators. None of the women legislators sent back the first round of questionnaire (although majority of them confirmed having received them), another round of questionnaire was sent. After persistent reminders, only 40 women legislators responded with filled in questionnaire. About the remaining women legislators, information was collected from the secondary sources available mainly in the published literature of UP Assembly secretariat. The analysis of the facts is presented in the following pages as in sequence of questions posed.

5.1 Socio-economic Background

To illustrate the main arguments of the study, the first question, who are the women leaders in UP? implies that what is the socio-economic, educational and other background of these women leaders in the state of UP. Women leaders for the purpose of this study mean the elected women legislators to the UP Assembly. The following background variables have been selected to study the first question. 1. Age of women at the time of entry to the Legislative Assembly; 2. Marital status; 3. Age at marriage;

4. Family size (number of children); 5. Occupation/Profession; 6. Education; 7. Caste/Community; and 8. Religion.

The findings on these variables are presented below :

Profile of the Women Legislators

Table 5.1: Distribution of Women Legislators by Age Group—Age at entry in to the Assembly

Sl. No.	*Age at Entering Assembly*	*Number of Women*	*% Age*
1	< 30 Years	15	15.79
2	30-39 Years	41	43.16
3	40-49 Years	28	29.47
4	50 Years and Above	11	11.58
	Total	95	100.00

Constitution prescribes a minimum age of 25 years to contest election for MLA and 30 years for the membership of legislative council. It remains silent about the upper age limit. Age profile of women legislators reveals that the maximum women entered into the assembly at the age of 30-39 years.

The bulk of women legislators, forty-three per cent (43.16%) was in the middle age group of 30-39 years as has already been stated above. It is little surprising since women of this age bracket are not fairly free from the domestic and family responsibilities. In fact, at this age, the children of most of the people are in the final school level and this period is critical for them, as they require constant guide and support from the family, particularly from the parents. However, the women legislators of this age group are mature and experienced and possibly less subject to the pitfalls of scandals and character assassination, which younger women are often subjected to.

A comparative study of age profile of women legislators from first to thirteenth Assembly (figures given in Appendix-6) reveals that the thirteenth and twelfth Assemblies have the highest representation of women of the age group 25-30 years. The youngest woman legislator was 25 years old in the Assembly. This indicates that comparatively more young women have been entering into politics at present than in the past.

There were only three women legislators in the Assembly above the age of 61 years who joined politics after their retirement from the government service. There were another three women legislators (3.15%) in the age group of 56-60 years.

Are marriage, child bearing and other responsibilities a hindrance to pursuit a political career? It is also often believed that woman's single status is more helpful to enter in active politics. The facts about marital status are presented in the following Table 5.2 :

Table 5.2 : Distribution of Women Legislators by Marital Status

Sl. No.		*No. of Women*	*% Age*
1	Unmarried	6	06.32
2	Married	62	65.26
3	Widow	27	28.42
	Total	95	100.00

In the present sample of 95 women legislators, it has been observed that only 6 women (6.32%) were unmarried and rest 89 were married at the time of their entry to the Assembly. Therefore, the majority of women legislators (93.70%) were married. Out of 89 married women, 27 were widows (28%).

Table 5.3: Distribution of Women Legislators by Age at Marriage

Sl. No.	*Age at Marriage*	*Number of Women*	*% Age*
1	< 15 Years	16	16.84
2	15-17 Years	35	36.84
3	18 Years and Above	38	40.00
4	Unmarried	6	6.62
	Total	95	100.00

The figures on age at marriage indicate that the majority of the women legislators (53.68 %) got married at the age of below 17 years. In fact, about 16.84 per cent were married very early below the age of 15 years.

Further details (given in Appendix 6) state that four legislators (about 4.21 per cent) were married as a child between the ages of 8-11 years, which is much below the prescribed marriageable age. Similarly, twelve women legislators (12.63%) were 12-15 years old at the time of their marriage and thus totally 16 women legislators were married as children. These legislators belonged to different castes, family backgrounds and educational levels (6 from SC, 4 from OBC and 6 from general castes). It may, therefore, be said that the child marriage was pervasive among all castes and in all the parts of UP.

Table 5.4 : Distribution of Women Legislators by Children

Sl. No.	*No. of Children*	*Number of Women*	*% Age*
1	3 and below	43	45.26
2	4-6	42	44.21
3	>6	4	04.21
4	Unmarried	6	06.32
	Total	95	100.00

Regarding the family size, it may be seen from Table 5.4 that about 44 per cent women legislators have 4-6 children, which shows higher family responsibilities and pursuing a political career. Of course, 45.26 per cent do have 3 or less children, 4 women legislators have even more than 6 children.

Table 5.5: Educational Background of Women Legislators in UP Assembly

Sl. No.	*Educational Level*	*Number of Legislators*	*%Age*
1	Under Matriculate	13	13.68
2	Under Graduates	32	33.69
3	Graduates and above	50	52.63
	Total	95	100.00

The above table 5.5 shows that only about 13.68 per cent of the women legislators were under-matriculates. The number of graduates and postgraduates are the highest, more than half (52.63 per cent). In the case of under-graduates, the position was far better than non-matriculates (33.70 per cent).

Further details (as given in Appendix-6) show that women legislators with doctoral degrees were indeed two (2.10 per cent). However, the graduates with LL.B. degrees and B.Ed. degrees (professionals) are about 18 per cent.

This indicates that the women teachers and lawyers have been increasingly joining politics than other professionals. Comparative analysis over the years shows that there is a better representation of women having higher level of education in present Assembly than in the past.

One interesting observation has been that the unmarried women legislators are highly educated. All the 6 unmarried women legislators are graduates and postgraduates having professional degrees like LL.B., B. Ed., M.Ed. and Ph.D.

Table 5.6 : Occupational Distribution of Women Legislators

Sl. No.	*Occupation*	*No. of Women Legislators*	*Percentage*
1	Agriculture	55	57.90
2	Teaching	9	09.47
3	Lawyer	8	8.42
4	Others	23	24.21
	Total	95	100.00

It may be seen that among the women legislators majority (58%) have agriculture as their occupation. Next to agriculture comes the category of political and social workers that is 28.40 per cent. Apart from these two, other professional groups, the teachers and lawyers have 9.47 and 8.42 per cent representation, respectively. There were three women legislators, who participated in active politics only after retirement from the government service.

As can be seen from the table above, representation of women from SCs category has been 25.26 per cent, higher than their reserved quota. Women from OBC are 13.68 per cent. However, there has been no representation of woman legislator from the ST category in the UP Assembly. It may be due to the fact that there is very small population of STs in the state of UP and only one seat, namely, Chakrota is reserved for ST, which has been always represented by a male legislator.

Table 5.7 : Caste Distribution of Women Legislators

Sl. No.	*Caste*	*Number of Women*	*% age*
1	Scheduled Caste	24	25.26
2	OBC	13	13.68
3	General	58	61.06
	Total	95	100.00

Religion as one of the variables seems to be insignificant in the present study because only three women legislators are Muslims and rest 92 are Hindus.

An attempt has been made to check the inter-relationship between the different variables and therefore following bi-variable tables have been prepared for Chi-square test.

Table 5.8: Relationship Between the Age at the Time of Entry to Assembly of Women Legislators and Their Caste

Sl. No.	*Age at the time of entry to Assembly*	*Scheduled Caste*	*OBC*	*General/ Others*	*Total*
1	<30 years	7	1	7	15
2	30-39 years	13	5	23	41
3	40-49 years	4	5	19	28
4	> 50 years	0	2	9	11
	Total	24	13	58	95

Note : Chi-square is not significant.

A significant number of women legislators from the SCs (about 29%) have entered into Assembly at below the age of 30 years while in case of general category, only 12 per cent women have entered in Assembly below 30 years. The same figure for OBC has been very low only at 7.7 per cent. Thus, comparatively more women from SCs have entered into Assembly at lower age than the women from OBC and general category.

Table 5.9: Relationship Between the Education of Legislators and Their Caste

Sl. No.	*Education*	*Scheduled Caste*	*OBC*	*General/ Others*	*Total*
1	Under Matric	4	4	4	12
2	Under Graduates	10	1	21	32
3	Graduates & above	10	8	33	51
	Total	24	13	58	95

This may be seen from Table 5.9 that the candidates from the general constituencies have higher educational qualifications as compared to those elected from the reserved constituencies. However, most of the SC women candidates are educated and at least high school passed. In fact, out of 24 women legislators belonging to the SC category, 10 (41.66%) were graduates and postgraduates and the equal numbers were of the undergraduates. Only 4 (16.66%) were under matric. The general level of higher education of OBC candidate is also higher.

Table 5.10: Relationship Between Education and No. of Times Elected

No. of Times Elected	*Under Matric*	*Under Graduate,*	*'Graduate & Above*	*Total*
One time	5	22	26	53
2-3 times	6	4	17	27
4 times and above	2	6	7	15
Total	13	32	50	95

The consecutively repeated representation of women legislators from their Assembly does not seem to be related to their level of education. It may be observed from table that there are 6 women legislators who are under-graduates but represented their constituencies more than four times. Similarly, 6 under matriculate women have represented their constituencies 2-3 times.

Over the years, the number of new entrants (without prior experience) has increased in the present Assembly in comparison to the previous Assemblies, wherein more experienced women legislators were elected. There were 156 women who had prior Assembly experience.

In the analysis, it may be said that some relationship does exist between the family background of women legislators and their participation in politics.

5.2 Emergence of Women Legislators

The second question is how they (women) have emerged as leaders. The basis, contributing factors and other circumstances of becoming leaders are described here on the basis of some general observations and the specific interviews conducted with them.

Most of the women leaders in the present study belong to the national political parties like the Congress, Samajwadi Party (SP), Bharatiya Janata Party (BJP) and Bahujan Samaj Party (BSP). These parties have been in power at one time or the other in the state of UP and most of them even at the Centre as well. Thus, the broader understanding and linkages are in the tune with the ideals of the senior party leaders and the emergence of women leadership, therefore, entirely depended upon the party high command. The high command often made the choice of women candidates for nominating them to contest the elections. Therefore, the emergence of state level leadership is also a show of loyalty either to the past or the present leadership of the party high command.

To study, "how women have become leaders?" following variables have been studied.

1. Family linkages; 2. Widow succession; 3. Political activist; 4. Social worker; and 5. Student activist.

Table 5.11: Contributing Factors in Emergence of Women Legislators in U.P.

Sl.No.	*Factors*	*Women*	*%age*
1	Family Linkage	21	22.10
2	Widow Succession	20	21.05
3	Political Activists	54	56.85
	Total	95	100.00

The political activists, social workers and student activists have been considered those who have become leaders by virtue of their talent and without having any family political history. This indicates achievement orientation of women rather than ascription.

Out of 95 women legislators 41 (43.15%) were having strong family linkages, which helped them to become leaders. They have come from the families where the father, brother and mother or husband was in active politics. Of course, there is majority of women (54 out of 95) who have joined politics because they were always interested in it. These were active members of student unions during their student life and members of employee's unions and joined full time active politics the moment they got a chance.

Such women leaders have higher education than their counterparts. Out of 54 women leaders who have been either social workers, student activists or political activists, 34 (63%) are graduates and above. Based on this observation, it may be said that the women legislators, who had emerged leaders without having any family linkages, were more educated than women with the political families.

In the sample, about 30 women legislators (31.58 per cent) were married to persons who were themselves political activists. Though they were elected in their individual capacities, their role was primarily supportive to their husbands who had leading positions in the politics of their respective areas. There are instances of politicized families where both the husband and wife were together active in politics of the area. However, there are clear indications that the involvement as also their election to Assembly was due to the influence of the male member.

The inter-relationships of above variables have shown that widow succession has been very pervasive in the UP politics. Out of 27 widows in the sample, as many as 20 (74%) were those who had been given tickets after the death of their husbands to fill in void. The widow succession has been without any other considerations than the husband's death and, therefore, no relationship does exist between their education, caste, family background and their emergence as leaders. Some more specific factors are observed through case studies.

5.3 Role of Women Legislators

The third question is "what role do they play?" means, their role as legislators and of the common women for the welfare of their family and the society at large. The state legislators are the focus of the positional power. They are considered to be the best source to get any type of social, economic, educational, rural and urban development works got done. They are beneficial for both, for their own caste people and for the larger society as well.

5.3.1 The women leaders have been playing a key role of linkages between the state and the people. Most of the general developmental works like water supply, schools, roads, electricity arrangements, etc. have easily been completed under the positional influence of the women legislators. Most of the women legislators have been able to provide such general facilities for the society during their terms. A few women legislators could also get the developmental work done at large scale due to their position as ministers. Though, there have been only one or two such women legislators at a time.

5.3.2 The role of scheduled caste women legislators for their own caste people has been in the form of social emulsion. Almost all the women legislators belonging to the scheduled castes have been demanding for the social justice in the legislature, at least for their own caste people. However, a joint action has never been seen in such cases. Their action is guided by the concerned party high command. Even if there is clear-cut case of social injustice, they do not dare to raise their voices against their party high command.

5.3.3 Another important role which the scheduled caste women legislators seem to play is that they have been helping their community to get grants from the various governmental agencies for the development of infrastructures in their constituencies and for the social welfare activities. They have helped in providing drinking water facilities and pucca roads in the residential areas of the scheduled castes.

5.3.4 It is admitted by some of the women legislators that they have tried to establish the big ventures in their constituencies where particularly the people of their own areas could have been absorbed or employed, but they were not succeeded because the same ventures were shifted in the constituencies of the more powerful male leaders.

5.3.5 The role of various women leaders appeared to draw the government aid for the construction of schools, libraries, girl hostels, community hall, social and religious functions, etc. A few have been able to improve the living conditions in their constituencies by improving conditions of streets, electricity and general social amenities in the rural areas. Many of them have been running their own schools, training institutions and centres for women and adult education.

5.3.6 Out of 95 women legislators, 55 (about 58%) have been directly or indirectly engaged in the social and welfare organizations. Though rest 40 have been mainly involved in the household works, simultaneously, they were participating in many of the social and religious activities in their constituencies without having direct affiliation to any of the social, welfare and religious organizations.

5.3.7 The position of women legislators based on their affiliation to the various organizations is given as under:

Table 5.12 : Women Legislators, Affiliation to Various Organizations

Sl. No.	*Organizations*	*SC*	*OBC*	*GEN*	*Total*
1	Adult education, training of rural women, educational institutes, etc.	6	1	11	18
2	NGOS, Social Welfare Voluntary Organizations, women empowerment, anti dowry, etc.	8	1	20	29
3	Active in party women wings	2		6	8
	Total	16	2	37	55

It can be seen from the table above that majority of women legislators 55 (i.e. 57.90 %) have been involved in the welfare activities of rural women, SCs and STs, widows and poor in their constituencies and working for improving the living conditions of the people by imparting training and education in them which ultimately resulting in increasing of their household incomes. The numerical distribution shows that out of the 55 women, a large segment (29) is active with NGOs and other organizations and a small portion (8) is holding positions in party wings for specific welfare organizations.

The above observations show that a segment of women legislators have been actively engaged in enhancing the educational and residential facilities, and welfare activities for women, girls, poor, widows and persons belonging to the SCs and STs.

5.3.8 General information also suggests that women leaders actually act as a linkage between the government and the common people. Some of the women legislators have been working for the rights and the welfare of SCs and STs, industrial workers and the government employees. They have been active in getting the reservation quota completely filled in the government as well as in the Boards, Corporations, Banks, etc. They have also been fighting against victimization of industrial workers.

5.3.9 Thus, to sum up the role of women leaders, it may be said that they have played a role for enhancement of education, self-employment, religious reforms, developing organizational skills for social security and justice, housing problems, water and sanitation problem, etc. The extent and the capacity of playing such roles largely depended upon their level of education, dynamism and on their experience as legislators.

5.4 Participation in the Assembly Proceedings

The fourth question is "what kind of issues do they raise in the Assembly?" The primary object of this question was to examine whether women legislators raised issues specific to the women problems only or also other general issues related to the problems to their constituencies and the state. But the level of their participation in the Assembly has been cursorily examined. An attempt has been made to find how many women legislators have been actively participating in the Assembly proceedings and the kind of issues being raised by them.

5.4.1 It has been observed that the visibility of women

legislators is very clear in the Assembly proceedings and deliberations. This is despite the fact that their numerical strength has been very low. A preliminary analysis of the available documented proceedings of the Assembly clearly indicate that though women legislators have been participating in the debates on various Bills and raising questions related to the local problems of their constituencies but this participation has been very low.

5.4.2 Based on the number of the questions women legislators have raised in the Assembly, they have been divided in three categories: (i) Very Active, (ii) Moderately Active, and (iii) Inactive/ Invisibles. The women legislators who have raised more than 25 questions during her complete five-year term have been considered very active participants; those who raised 5 and above but less than 25 questions considered moderate; and less than 5 questions considered as inactive/invisible participants. Their position with regard to their involvement in the Assembly proceed-ings has been given in Table 5.12 below.

Table 5.12: Degree of Participation of Women Legislators in the Assembly Proceedings

Sl. No.	*Participation*	*No. of Women*	*Percentage*
1	Very Active	36	37.90
2	Moderately Active	27	28.42
3	Inactive/ Invisible	32	33.68
4	Total	95	100.00

The above table shows that a little more than 1/3rd (37.90%) women have been very active in the Assembly proceedings while 28 per cent women legislators were moderately participating and one-third (33.68) were invisible.

A certain set of laid down legislatory rules and procedures govern both men and women legislators in the Assembly while raising issues. However, owing to their weak numerical strength, women remained in disadvantageous position.

5.4.3 An analysis of ninth Assembly* (1985-89) documented proceedings may be presented as an illustration, which had the maximum number of women legislators (7.30%). Total eleven sessions of the ninth Assembly (1985-89) were held during its full term. Total 137 Bills were introduced, out of 137 discussions held under the rules 301, 491, 51, 52 and 56, women participated in only 10, which is merely 7.30 per cent. Thus, their participation numeri-cally appears in the same ratio as their strength. However, on the ten occasions, only five women repeatedly participated and, therefore, their participation comes out to less than their numerical strength.

The analysis of the Bills and participation of the women legislators in debates and discussions year-wise is given below.

Table 5.13: Women Legislators Participation in Ninth Assembly Discussions

Year	*No. of Sessions*	*No. of Bills*	*No. of Women*	*%Age*
1985	2	31	3	09.67
1986	2	32	3	09. 37
1987	3	23	4	17.40
1988	2	21	Nil	-
1989	2	30	Nil	-
Total	11	137	10	7.30

Source: UP Assembly Documentation Section-Proceedings.

Out of the total 31 discussions in 1985, women participated in only three, which is only 9.6 per cent. Only three women legislators participated in discussions held in 1986 wherein total 32 discussions were held. Thus, it may be seen from the table that the position of women legislators in discussions on Bills has been very low.

* Only Ninth and Thirteenth Assemblies have been considered for consulting proceedings particularly for discussions on Bills. 13th Assembly is the last Assembly taken as a case currently available and 9th Assembly was selected because women have had the largest representation. Considering the large numbers and huge documents, the whole proceedings, from first to the last Assembly could not be consulted and also it was not required as it may be an another topic for the research).

Table 5.14: Women Legislators Participation in Thirteenth Assembly Discussions

Year	*No. of Sessions*	*No. of Bills*	*No. of Women*	*%Age*
1996	Nil	Nil	Nil	Nil
1997	2	25	4	16.00
1998	4	27	2	07.40
1999	2	37	3	8.10
Total	8	89	9	10.11

5.4.4 The position in the 13th Assembly is presented in Table 5.14.

Out of 89 Bills during 1996-99, women participated in nine discussions only which works out to be about 10 per cent. Similarly, a glance at the levels of participation of women legislators on Bills moved and considered in the Assembly for the period 1952-93* too confirms the very low percentage (in some of the sessions nearly absence) of women in actual deliberations. A comparative study of the old and the recent past Assemblies shows that women were relatively actively involved in the context of the Bills in the 1st, 2nd and 3rd Assemblies**, however, this involvement has remained glaringly low in 9th-13th Assemblies.

The above information was collected from the documented proceedings of 9th-13th Assemblies about the lower participation of women legislators. This was also discussed with legislators during the course of their interviews. They were asked not merely to respond to the near non-involvement of women in Assembly proceedings over the various sessions of the Assembly in the post-independence period but also to tell about what the present situation is since the proceedings of the ongoing Assembly have not been completely documented as yet.

5.4.5 Contrary to the expectations, that lower participation being primarily a factor of gender discrimination, majority of women legislators were emphatic that their presumed lower participation is more a function of their low numerical strength

* Analysis of all the Assembly debates could not be worked out due their large numbers and huge voluminous documents but the author has had a cursory glance through all the proceedings randomly.

** This finding is indicated on the basis of random glance.

than gender discrimination. The Assembly governed by the certain set of procedural rules and regulations, which are universally applicable to each member independent of their sex. Moreover, by and large, such decisions as who would speak on which issue in the house are taken by the various political parties in the Assembly.

Yet within these procedural constraints women are at a disadvantage because of their low numerical strength. The fewer the women are, the lesser chances they get to speak. There are exceptions, but they more or less prove to be the rule. The women who have been 'visible' or prominent are a selected few.

5.4.6 The issues raised by the women in the Assembly vary from the poor state economy to disasters caused by the natural calamities, management of food grains, problem of unemployment, drinking water and housing problems, poor school management, violence, atrocities on women and SCs, murder in the constituency, etc. and the small local issues related to the a town or village.

The legislators of the sample when asked about the kind of issues being raised gave wide-ranging answers. Whereas most of the active legislators, out of 36, 30 (83.33 %) from all the parties and different parts of the state said that they had often been raising issues concerning to their own constituencies. This is in fact also evident from the documented proceedings. Another small segment of 4 (11.11 %) active participants mentioned labour related issues. Yet another 2 old timers from the BJP mentioned specific problems of crimes in the western belt of UP, particularly in Meerut and Saharanpur commissioneries and water, sanitation, hygiene, education and labour related issues in eastern parts of the state. They have also mentioned matters specific to women atrocities.

5.4.7 During the interviews, women legislators as well as the controlled small group of male legilators emphatically expressed the views that in the Assembly women specific issues were being raised by men legislators and were, therefore, not 'ghettoized' in terms of raising only women-specific issues. In fact, the legislators were insistent that the tendency to limit women legislators, concerns to only women specific issues might harm the cause rather than further it since women's issues were not merely women's concerns but men as well.

Despite the fact that women legislators have been raising a

variety of issues, the number of such women is very few. Moreover, as far as the responses on issues are concerned, on the floor of the Assembly, by and large, women legislators cut across the party lines and join hands on issues relating to violence and atrocities inflicted on women.

5.4.8 On the other general issues, however, women legislators often toe their respective party lines. Sometimes, this is the case even when issue of violence on a woman, but has happened in the constituency represented by the ruling senior leaders and incumbent ministers of the ruling party. In such a situation, the ruling party women members take a stand more on party lines than the treating it as women's issues.

This brings to the related aspect of women legislator taking a different stand than their party on a particular issue on the floor of the Assembly, especially women's issue. There have been instances when women took such a stand and some of the legislators even gave instances from their own experiences. There have, however, been situations when women members were forced to take a stand detrimental to the cause of women. This does not indicate that women legislators have not taken a stand different from their parties on a controversial issue, specifically if it is one relating to women.

5.4.9 In this context the frequency and incidence of raising issues, moving resolutions etc. appears to be related to the age, experience and familiarity of women legislators with the legislatory rules and procedures, the experience of the women legislators both in terms of 'time' (for how long she has been actively engaged in this field) as also her exposures to political activities from the grassroots level. For instance, in the present sample, 36 women legislators who have actively participated in the Assembly are those who have consecutively represented the Assembly for 3-4 times. This indicates that legislators gain familiarity with the rules and procedures of Assembly and exposures to the debates with the pace of time.

5.5 Hindrance/Obstacles

The fifth question is about the hindrance/obstacles faced by the women legislators while entering into politics.

5.5.1 Except one or two legislators, all have denied any difficulty or resistance to their entry in politics. During the course of interviews held with them, two legislators, however, categorically said that their children initially were not happy and objected to their entry in politics. Some of them have faced mild problems and also were manhandled during election campaigns and other visits to their constituencies, as they have narrated some instances of violence, inflicted upon them, during the interviews.

5.5.2 There were few instances where women legislators clearly pointed out that their children were reluctant and were not allowing them to join political life. There were many other instances, where women were born into political families but could join politics only in their 30s and 40s, since they had to pursue their family duties as the first priority.

By and large, women are treated well on the floor of the House and to quote a male legislator 'women have sobering effect on their male colleagues'. Thus, it may be concluded that most of the women legislators have not faced any difficulty in entering politics. Although, one or two of them have confirmed the initial mild resistance from their family, particularly from their children, but majority of women legislators have denied any hindrance from family or otherwise to their entry into politics and pursuing their political carrier further.

6

CASE STUDIES

This chapter includes a few case studies of some women legislators in terms of their entry into politics, their socio-economic background, their involvement in party decision-making processes and participation in legislature proceedings. The details of seven women legislators as case studies are described focusing mainly on the aspects of the proposed questions raised in the problem of the present study. Efforts have been made to arrive at findings and establishing relationships with the questions in each case and then summing up of those clearly depicting their relationships.

6.1 Case Study–I

Ms Mayawati, popularly known in the Bahujan Samaj Party (BSP) as "Bahin ji", was born in 1956 and is now 46 years old and unmarried. She started her political career 19 years back when she was only 27 years of age. She is the first woman from amongst scheduled castes who became the Chief Minister thrice of the largest state like UP. Although her tenure as Chief Minister was too short, only of total eleven months to put together (Ist two terms) but she has achieved many milestones in her political carrier, which other politicians could not achieve in life time career.

She was bron in a Jatav, scheduled caste (Dalit) family. Her father was a resident of the village Badalpur in Bulandshahar district of U.P., who eventually settled in Delhi due to his government service. Ms. Mayawati was born and brought up in Delhi and she completed her studies in Delhi only. She graduated from University of Delhi and later did her B.Ed. She then joined LL.B. degree. She wanted to be an Indian Administrative Service (IAS) officer to serve the Dalit class of the society.

Her father was a great follower of Dr. Ambedker and was a

frequent visitor to Dr. Ambedker Bhawan, particularly on the day of celebration of the birthday of Dr. Ambedker wherein many politicians and intellectuals use to speak about the sacrifices and achievements of Dr. Ambedker. He always used to carry Ms Mayawati along on all such occasions. She was highly impressed and influenced by the teachings of Dr. Ambedkar.

In 1977, when Janata Party was in power at the Centre, there was a three-day seminar in Constitutional Club, Delhi, organized by the Janata Party on "Remove Caste" where Ms Mayawati was invited as one of the speakers. Socialist leader late Shri Rajnarayan was convening function and repeatedly using "Harijan" word while addressing people belonging to the scheduled castes. When Ms Mayawati was invited to the stage to deliver her speech she said that "on one hand, Shri Rajnarayan ji is talking about removal of castes while calling people of scheduled castes as Harijans on the other. There is no word like "Harijan" in the Indian Constitution. The leader like Rajnarayan would never allow the removal of the caste system in the country. Therefore, the conference on "Remove Caste" seems to me cheating on the people of scheduled castes. The people of oppressed castes sitting there appreciated this kind of bold statement. After the conference, people belonging to the lower castes gathered at a place wherein workers of BSP unit of Delhi were also present. The BSP workers were so much impressed by the views of Ms Mayawati that they went to meet her next day at her residence. During the discussion, they mentioned about the BSP movement and its founder Shri Kansi Ram and invited her to join BSP movement. Kanshi Ram was also told about Ms Mayawati and her flaring speech. Later, he listened to her in one or two public meetings. He was impressed by her thoughts and one day went to meet her at her residence. The BSP workers accompanied him. All the members of her family were present in the house and she was preparing for her IAS examination at that time. This was the first meeting between Mayawati and Kanshi Ram. Looking at the heap of books, Kanshi Ram asked Mayawati, what does she want to be after her studies. Mayawati replied that she wanted to be a Collector and serve the people of the oppressed classes. Kanshi Ram said that she couldn't serve them even if she succeed to be a Collector because a Collector is a puppet of the ruling party in the state and had to work as per the direction from the political masters of that party. Mayawati realised that if the society had to be served at a larger scale, she had to be a leader of the society and not the Collector. This was the turning point in her life and she joined BSP movement. She decided to join politics and BSP party as well. Initially, her father opposed her joining the BSP movement. He thought the BSP movement might not pick up and his daughter might fail in life. He suggested to play safe and to go for a lucrative government job. If at all she had to go for a political career she should join some already successful party and not the one, which is yet to be launched. According to Mayawati, she discussed this matter with Kanshi Ram and he told her that it is a matter of ideology to him; it should be a matter of ideology for her also. Success or failure comes later, firmly told Kanshi Ram. She opted for the BSP movement. Prior to her active political career, she was a teacher in Delhi Education Department from 1977 to 1984.

BSP was established in 1984 and in 1989 by-election, Mayawati was elected as first MP of the BSP from Bijnore parliamentary constituency. This is how Mayawati entered into active politics. As per the statement of Mr. Kanshi Ram, keeping in mind the opposition of her father, he decided to give her more and more opportunities to exhibit her talent. The seniors in the BSP movement did not like this. They started opposing her. The more problems were created for her.

During the years of 1982-83, the platform of Dalit Soshit Samaj Sangarsh (DS-4) was used in a big way. Many experiments were conducted by using platform of DS-4. During these experiments, she got much exposure and opportunities to show her talent. This kind of chances created jealousy among the seniors in the movement. They started opposing her vehemently. In such an atmosphere BSP was launched on 14th April in 1984. BSP brought more opportunities. She prepared Muzaffar Nagar district and fought 1984 Lok Sabha from Kairana Lok Sabha seat. Out of all the BSP candidates, all over India, she got the highest number of votes. This created more jealousy amongst the seniors. In 1985, she prepared for the Bijnore Lok Sabha seat and she was nominated as candidate during the byelection. By securing 65000 votes, she made it a triangular fight. The success she achieved in this election created more problems for her. The senior colleagues of her in BSP could not tolerate her rise (Akhter, 1999: 2). She told that they tried to put pressure on Kanshi Ram to curtail opportunities given to her. On the refusal of the same, most of the seniors had left the movement, started on their own. But none of them who opposed the rise of her is visible today. Whereas Mayawati has become a success as Chief Minister of the largest state of India.

In 1993, first time there was alliance between SP and BSP in UP and Mulayam Singh was elected as the Chief Minister. But the alliance could not last long and after 18 months, the BSP withdrew its support to Mulayam Singh government, which was then reduced to the minority. The BJP and the Congress supported BSP and Mayawati was elected as the Chief Minister. She thus became the first youngest Scheduled Caste (Dalit) woman Chief Minister in India. Again in 1997, in alliance with BJP and in 2002 as well, she was elected Chief Minister for the third time. Her tenure as Chief Minister, in first two terms has been very short but she has always been on the national scene of Indian politics. In twelfth Lok Sabha in 1998, she won from Akbarpur reserved constituency and in 1999 election, again re-elected from the same constituency. She has been conferred many national and international awards for promoting social justice to backward classes and Dalits.

This case study shows that this woman leader (legislator) is quite young, dynamic, well educated coming from a very ordinary lower middle class scheduled caste family. She is a life member of the BSP. In fact she is one of the founder members and General Secretary of this party. She has emerged as a leader by virtue of her talent as she had no political family background. She has won first election as an MP of her party. She has not only been successful in winning parliamentary seat but also became the Chief Minister of the largest state of India thrice.

Initially, there was opposition from her family for her entering into politics, as her father wanted her to be an I.A.S. officer. She also has to face strong opposition within the party from her seniors for the opportunities used by her. She feels that women are not easily accepted in party organization. She takes strong exception that women should be treated at par with men and there should not be any discrimination. She said that the persons entering into politics should be properly trained so that they could effectively participate in the party activities. She suggested that political training should start from grassroots level. Women should be told and made to understand how they can bring change in society. Hard work and integrity are the only ways to succeed in life. She has admitted that because of her family's non-political background she had to work hard to make a place for herself in the party politics.

She is deeply influenced by Dr. Ambedkar. She created many parks and statues of Ambedkar during her tenure as the Chief Minister, which of course were not admired and appreciated by the opposition. She preaches the teachings of Dr. Ambedkar and asks her brethren to achieve the distinction of a scholar like him. The scholarly personality, hard working spirit and a confident attitude of Dr. Ambedkar have impressed her much to become a leader. She favours his ideology of social transformation.

She started many new schemes like Ambedkar Gram Yojana, administrative reforms, police reforms, rural development programme, etc. There were many other schemes for improving the socio-economic conditions of scheduled castes and backward class people. Check on the atrocities on SCs was her prime concern. Although construction of hostels for girls, granting them scholarships, eradication of child prostitution were part of her first budget speech in the Assembly as Chief Minister. Apparently, there is no other women specific issue, which was taken up by her in Assembly or raised in the Parliament.

6.2 Case Study–II

The second case study is about another woman legislator who belonged to Bhartiya Janata Party (BJP). Prior to entering active politics, she was a teacher. However, right from her school days she was associated with the socialist movement. The initial inspiration to enter politics was from her uncle. Her father too was in politics. After her marriage there was no difficulty for her because her husband was also active in politics.

Smt. Prabha Diwedi, who is 66 years old now, joined politics after her retirement from the government service and was elected as legislator in the by-election, which was completed on 29th May 1997. She is graduate and a trained teacher. She is a widow. Her husband died pre-mature death. She was married to late Shri Braham Dutt Diwedi who was a social worker and an active politician. Her father, Shri L.K. Dubey, was a resident of Shadi Nagar, district Farukhabad who worked in the state government, and belonged to the lower middle class. Smt. Prabha Diwedi has worked as Principal of Govt. Girls' Inter College, Basic Education Officer, and Professor in S.C. R.T., Lucknow. From 27th March, 1997 to December 1997, she was Minister of Labour and Services in the Cabinet of Ms Mayawati and also was the Minister of Labour in the Kalyan Singh Ministry.

She came from a middle class educated family. Her husband and father were both in active politics though none of them ever fought any election. Although she joined politics only after her retirement from the government job, but she has a political background wherein her husband groomed Farukhabad constituency and after his death she was nominated as BJP candidate from Farukhabad and won the same with a good margin.

It shows that she is well connected to a political family. She came into politics through fighting an election. She has to play a dual role, one for the public life and other of single widow mother of her three children which she find a uphill task. One important aspect of her political life has been that she was made Minister in the both Mayawati and Kalayan Singh cabinets though she was elected for the first time to the Assembly. This was due to her talent and experience in the service life.

She fights for the problems of the local people. She has taken up many issues of atrocities on women in the Assembly. She admitted that very few women are vocal in the Assembly. She also raised issues related to the various problems like labour, television and industries, etc. She started many social work related to the women empowerment such as women literacy and their income generation. She feels that the family responsibilities were hindrance in her way to enter the politics. After the death of her husband, she wanted to participate in politics but due to responsibility of the children on her shoulders alone, she continued to be in the government service. She organised election campaigns for the party in the state. She enjoys a commanding position within her party. She raised funds for the party. She stressed that one could draw the attention of the speaker of Assembly only if one is sincere and is a person of integrity.

She was of the opinion that women should be educated and trained before they enter politics. They should be given more responsibility. They should join politics in larger numbers in order to put strong resistance to communalisation and criminalisation of politics. One very interesting factor that came out was that she was against reservation of seats for women and felt that women should not be given any minority status because they were second to none.

6.3 Case Study–III

This is the case study of a leading woman legislator, Kumari Urmilla Agnihotri from Sauri constituency of Etah district. She is 62 years old now and was elected to UP Assembly first time in 1980 at the age of 40. She was again elected for the second time in 1985 and both the times Congress (I) party tickets. But she was very much active in politics in her younger days. She has graduated from Agra University and completed her LL.B. from Lucknow University. She was a practicing advocate before she joined active politics. She is unmarried. Her father, late Shri Pundit Rewatilal Agnihotri, had expired when she was only 14 years. Her mother brought her up. She belonged to a lower middle class conservative family. She was jailed twice in 1977-78 for 15 days in connection with Kans Ganj Barahdari Jhanda Andolan and opposing Smt. Indira Gandhi's arrest.

She joined All India Congress as a life member in the year 1957 at the age of 17 years and has been an active Congress worker since then. She became member of UP Congress Committee in 1960 at the age of 20 and remained member until 1964. After that she has been the member of various committees and worked on many party posts in the Congress including Member, All India

Congress Committee (1965-72); Member, District Board Etah (1963); Member, Regional Catering Committee, Railway; Coordinator, U.P. Minority and Backward Class, etc. She was elected unopposed Deputy Chairperson of Collectorate Bar, Etah; Member, Working Committee of Etah Bar Association, President, B.R. Junior High School, Etah; President, All India Post and Telegraphy Workers Association, etc.

She is an active member of the Mahila Congress, the women's wing of the Congress party. She was the National Convenor of the Mahila Congress and contributed a lot in drafting the constitution of the Mahila Congress. She raised a number of women's issues and got them included into the Congress party manifesto. She openly advocated 30 per cent reservation of seats for women in different political bodies and state legislatures. She was also a member of the campaign committee both at the state and at the national level and has suggested names of female candidates for elections and also for different position in the party organisation. Apart from the women related issues, she expressed her concern for other socially relevant issues and problems.

As a representative of her constituency in the Assembly, she has raised issues specific to her area, i.e. Sauri Ganj, district Etah as well as those of general concern in the Assembly. She takes keen interest in all Assembly proceedings and never had any problems in putting her viewpoint convincingly on the Assembly floor. She has moved several resolutions successfully in the Assembly. She showed concern for the casual attitude of men legislators towards women related issues. However, she contended that all women legislators should unite and extend their support on women specific issues irrespective of their affiliation to different political parties. She stressed that women legislators should not be given special privileges and there should not be any discrimination between women and men legislators.

As stated above, she is of the opinion that men and women should be treated at par. Neither should there be any discrimination nor any special privilege granted to women. But she could feel the indifferent and casual attitude of her male colleagues in the Assembly towards women related issues. This she does not appreciate. She rather feels that all male legislators should strongly support women related issues. Given an opportunity women can do equally well as men.

She expressed her concern for the criminalisation and communalisation of politics. A mass awareness by media and electoral reforms can help in educating the people to counter the existing social evils. She suggested reservation of seats in elections and jobs for women for at least 25 years and stressed that the need for women to stand up as equals and participate fully in the national building process.

6.4 Case Study–IV

Here is a case of a women belonging to the Indian National Congress who joined active politics because of circumstances. She is an agriculturist by occupation. Smt. Santosh Kumari Pathak, born in 1947 in Data Ganj in Badaun district, UP. She is now 55 years of age. She was married to Shri Akhilesh Chander Pathak in 1960 at the age of 13 years only and has three children. Her father late Shri Trivani Sahay Sharma was an active politician. He was an M.L.A. in the fifth UP Assembly (1969) and was murdered in May 1971. It was only after her father's death that she was persuaded to join active politics and contest the election. After the death of her father, she was given ticket in 1972 byelection. And she was elected from Data Ganj on Indian National Congress ticket. She was then only 25 years old. She had no support from her in-laws because they felt that being a young woman she would not be able to face the challenges. However, her husband supported her. She contested her first election in 1972 and won. Again, in 1974 general Assembly elections, she was elected. Third and fourth time, she was elected in 1980 and 1989 general elections respectively.

She had some experience in the public services and exposure to many social and educational institutions of her district right from the days of her father. She used to attend several social functions with her father when he was an M.L.A. Therefore, she was a familiar face of her areas. She was the youngest woman legislator when elected to Assembly for the first time in 1972. She also became Member of U.P. Congress Committee in 1972.

In the year 1977-78, she along with her family was arrested and jailed with Mrs. Indira Gandhi during Congress movement against the arrest of Mrs. Gandhi. On the violation of IPC 144 in 1978, she was jailed in district jail Badaun for one month and was also fined rupees one hundred for the same offence. She has been a member of many legislative consultative committees during 1980-85. She is deputy chairperson of Gangadeen Inter College, Goora and Bareilly. She takes keen interest in the women welfare activities and educational expansion. She is running an Inter college in her area.

She always enjoyed the confidence of other party colleagues and their cooperation too. She visits her constituency frequently. She raised women-related issues/problems on the floor of the House. She has also been raising problems of her constituency, especially those related to labour, women and children, health care and education. She feels that women should be more educated, which would help them to act effectively in the party organisation.

She advocates 50 per cent reservation of seats for women in the different legislative and elected bodies since women constitutes almost 50 per cent of the total population of the country. She emphasises that there should be no discrimination between men and women and that they should be treated equally in all realms of life.

6.5 Case Study–V

Here is the case study of another woman legislator from INC who belongs to the higher middle class family and has been Minister in the Centre and in the State as well. Smt. Sushila Rohatigi was born in 1921 in Allahabad. Her father late Pundit Kapil Dev was a famous lawyer of Allahabad High Court. She studied in Allahabad University. She had also worked as Lecturer of History in 1945-46 in Allahabad University. She was married in inter-caste in 1947 to Shri Mahendra Rohatigi, the founder of Hind Chemicals Limited. Her father in-law, Dr. Jawahar Lal Rohatigi was a Member of Parliament and State Minister in U.P. Government. She has five children, two sons and three daughters.

Sushila Rohatigi was Minister in the Ninth U.P. Assembly in the cabinet of Shri Vir Bahadur Singh and in the cabinet of Shri Narayan Dutt Tiwari. She has been working on various posts of All India Mahila Congress Committee (AIMCC) since long. She was first elected to the Vidhan Sabha in the year 1962 on INC ticket from Kanpur-V constituency. She was coordinator of 28th AIMCC Session held in Kanpur.

She has been working for improvement of the living conditions of people in the slum areas. She is the member of various social organisations and holding many posts. She is member of Ladies Craft College Management Committee, Hindu Orphanage House Management Committee, Federation of Child Welfare Kanpur, Rural Women Association of U.P., Kanpur Congress Committee, Kanpur Municipal Committee, etc. and the Vice-Chairperson of District Council of Child Welfare, Kanpur. She is the co-ordinator of the committee of Bhartiya Vidhya Bhawan Kala Kendra and Ravindra Memorial Committee. She has visited Shri Lanka in 1958 as one of the member of Representative Group to attend Asian-African Conference for Women in Colombo. She is author of a book entitled "Bapu Ne Kaha Tha" (Bapu had told) and has written many articles in various national magazines. Her article "Dairy—An Eye Opener" was appreciated and admired by the people.

She has been associated with the social work right from her childhood days. There was no difficulty for her entering politics because her father, her father in-law and husband have been in the politics. She has been actively participating in the women's wing of Congress Party and worked as office-bearer of the same. She visited her constituency quite often and was involved in the day-to-day social activities in her areas.

She raised issues mostly related to the local problems, particularly of mill mazdoors, problem of labour after closure of Jute Mill and Flour Mill in Kanpur, FCI Gorakhpur Fertilizer Plant closure, family welfare, child health and care, poor condition of roads, lack of infrastructure facilities in Kanpur, hospital working conditions, teacher, college and school related problems, etc. She also moved no confidence motion against cabinet and actively participated in the debate of no confidence motion.

She is of the view that there should not be any distinction between women and men while allocating the party work, portfolio or any other important assignment, but feels that there is discrimination against women at every stage. She is concerned about this attitude of her senior party colleagues. Although she does not want any special privilege for women in Assembly or Parliament, but advocated for 30 per cent reservation of seats for women in different political parties, state legislatures and in the Parliament.

As already stated above, she has been Minister of State in the Centre for about a year and twice in the ninth state Assembly in the cabinets of Shri Vir Bahadur Singh and Shri Narayan Dutt Tiwari. She did not get an opportunity to choose the portfolio of her choice. Rather the party leader assigned it. According to her, she could have "perhaps" performed better had she been given a portfolio of her choice. But at the same time she confirmed that there is always a place for initiative as far as exercise of power is concerned. She also worked towards bringing changes in terms of policy decisions of the party.

6.6 Case Study–VI

Here is the case study of a woman who changed her party from Congress to Janata Party. She won on Congress tickets continuously three times, first time in 1974, second time in 1980 and third time in 1985 from Etawah constituency. She changed her party in 1989 election and contested election on Janata Party ticket supported by Mulayam Singh.

Smt. Sukhada Mishra was born in Daulatpur in an upper caste Brahaman family in 1947. She is 55 years of age now and was 33 years when elected first in 1974. Her father Shri Durdarshak Trivedi was well known social worker of Daulatpur, Etahwa district. She was married to Shri Shashikant Mishra who later became an I.A.S officer. Her father has large holding of agricultural land and was known one of the biggest landlords of his village. She is a science graduate and has two children, a son and a daughter.

She was chairperson of various welfare committees during her husband's posting as District Magistrate (DM). She used to attend and address many social gatherings, which became a source of inspiration for her to join active politics. She decided to join Congress party. Initially, her in-laws and husband resisted her idea of entering active politics. As per her statement, her husband was susceptible of her success and had an apprehension that she may create problems for his carrier. But later, she was able to convince both her in-laws and husband.

She was political prisoner in Lucknow Jail for violation of I.P.C. 151. She was Energy Minister in the cabinet of Shri Narayan Dutt Tiwari and also was Minister for Rural Development and Panchayat Raj in the cabinet of Shri Mulayam Singh. She is a member of All India Social Welfare Board and Child Welfare Board. She has been the manager of International Centre of Studies and has visited many countries like America, England and France.

She is firm on her opinion that sycophancy is very much persistent in the Indian politics, particularly in Congress party. According to her, she left the Congress because she could not tolerate sycophancy. She admitted that though she still likes the ideology of Congress but she has to leave the party as none bothers about her views or sentiments at the top level of party wherein major decision are taken. She has no regret about her decision of changing party from Congress to Janata and is happy about the things as they have turned up in U.P. politics, particularly the fall of the INC in U.P. as she has correctly apprehended.

She is also in favour of the women reservation in all political parties at various levels and in the government jobs. She thinks that the women are not taken seriously in the party organisation and also at the floor of the House. Similar statement was given by another woman selected for the case study earlier. She thinks that it is a very bad attitude of the senior men colleagues.

She raised issues related to the local problems and the general development of infrastructural facilities in her constituency. She has never raised an issue related to the women specially as she thinks that it is a larger issue and should be handled at the Centre level. As stated above, she has also expressed her views, as earlier expressed by other women legislators, that men and women should be treated at par. Neither should there be any discrimination nor any special privilege granted to women. But she could feel the indifferent and casual attitude of her male colleagues in the Assembly towards women related issues. This she does not appreciate. She rather feels that all male legislators of the assembly should strongly support women related issues.

6.7 Case Study–VII

This is the case study of the oldest woman, 93 years of age now, who has been participating in the active politics since her younger days. She was the first woman elected as Member of U.P. Legislative Council in 1937 in pre-independence era. Smt. Kudesia Begum, also known as Begum Azaz Rasul was born in 1909 in Lahore. She belongs to the Nawab family (Royal Family). Her father Sir Zulfikar Ali Khan was the famous Nawab of Hardoi. She was married in another Nawab family to Nawab Syed Azaz Rasul in 1930 at the age of 20 years. She took active part in freedom struggle.

She had her education in Convent of Jesus and Marry, Shimla and Queen Mary's College, Lahore. She has four children, two each sons and daughters. She had no difficulty in entering politics. In the pre-independence, when U.P. Legislative Council was established, she was the first woman to be elected for the same.

She was elected unopposed to U.P. Legislative Council and was Deputy Chairperson of U.P. Legislative Council from 1937 to 1939. She was consecutively elected to Legislative Council in pre-independence era from 1937 to 1952. She was Member of the Indian Constituent Assembly in 1946-50 and was Leader of the Opposition, U.P. Legislative Council in 1950-52. She represented Assembly from Lucknow constituency continuously during 1957-68. She was also Member of Parliament (MP), Rajya Sabha during 1952-56.

She was elected to Vidhan Sabha first time in the by-election in 1969 on Congress ticket. She was Minister in 1969 in the Cabinets of Shri C.B. Gupta and in T. N. Singh. She resigned from cabinet in 1971. She was again elected in 1977 from Sandila constituency as an independent candidate and again in 1980 and 1985 elections, she won on the Congress ticket.

She was Vice-President, Uttar Pradesh Women's Food Council and Indian Red Cross Society. She has been the Member of various committees, prominently included Central and Executive Committee of Tuberculosis Association of India and St. John's Ambulance, Central Haz Committee, U.P. Children Committee, U.P. State Duffer in Fund Committee, U.P. Zamidari Abolition Committee, U.P. Medical and Public Health Reorganisation Committee, Primary and Secondary Education Committee and U.P. Control Enquiry Committee.

She is quite old and has all old aged related alignments. She was quite cooperative otherwise during her interview. She strongly advocated for women reservation in the assemblies, parliament and all local and government bodies. She wanted special provisions for women in assemblies and parliament so their participation could be increased. She stressed the need for women education because she thinks that this is one area where women are lagging far behind. Particularly, she was sad about the poor education level among women belonging to the minority community. She opined that the lower representation of Muslim women in active politics was due to their lower education.

She said that her men colleagues were very cooperative to her in the Assembly and in Parliament as well. She has no experience of any indifference attitude of them anytime, anywhere. She raised whole range of issues related to the local problems and in fact nothing specific to women related problems. She feels that this is one area wherein Central Government intervention is needed. There is a need of a complete, concrete and comprehensive gender sensitisation programme at the national level, according to her. She was sad about the increasing of atrocities against women and current incidents of rape along with other forms of public humiliation. She is also of the view that the empowerment process encompasses several mutually reinforcing components but begins with and is supported by economic indepedence. Therefore, she wants women to be economically independent and this in her view, is possible only if women have knowledge and awareness of one's self and society, and of personal needs, health issues, legal rights, technological innovations, and availability of social and economic resources and how take advantage of them. This all can be learned once women are highly educated, according to her.

She came from the royal family and has no resistance from her parents or in-laws while entering into active politics. Her father was also an active politician. She was actively involved in the development of her constituency and she headed many local social organisations, which were active in the area of women and child health care and welfare. She got opened girls school in her constituency Sandila. She was also given many assignments in her party, which she completed successfully.

She was initially elected Member, Constituent Assembly from Muslim League, United Province. She resigned in 1969 from the T. N. Singh cabinet owing some differences in the party ideology and contested election in 1974 as an independent candidate that she won. Later, she again joined INC in 1980 and won two consecutive elections in 1980 and 1985 on Congress ticket. She owes her successful political career to her husband and in-laws who cooperated her in rearing children. She admitted that without their cooperation, it would not have been possible for her to build a political carrier and reach where she is now. She feels that a woman free from household responsibilities can spare more time than a woman having family responsibilities. She seems to be satisfied in her life and enjoying her retirement.

6.8 Summing up of Case Studies

All these case studies show that most of the women legislators came from middle class families and majority of them have political family background. They emerged as leaders through electoral process and many of them were elected to the Assembly three-four times consecutively. This shows their popularity in their constituencies. They have to play duel roles, one as a leader in the public service and other as responsible wife and mother. This increases their burden and some feels that owing the family responsibilities, they are not able to do justice to their role of a politician.

All these case studies show the attitude of women legislators towards the role of women in politics, their status in the political party and their opinion and suggestions for certain remedial measures to be undertaken in order to improve the role of women in political process. Most of them felt that women related issues are discussed casually and importance paid to such issue is marginal. This is primarily because women are not represented in large numbers in different elected bodies either at local level, at state level or at national level. They, therefore, stressed the need for at least 30 per cent reservation for women in the various political forums and political bodies both at local and state levels.

Many of them suggested that women should be properly educated and their awareness should be increased so that they can effectively participate in the political process, particularly in the decision making process. Many women legislators of our sample belong to families having political background, as already stated above, they have established themselves in the party organisation with the support of their parents or their spouses. Therefore, it suggests that women should be motivated, politically educated and should be encouraged to participate in the political process.

Although on the floor of the House they raise various issues but most of them seem to be more concerned with the issues related to the women. Irrespective of their party affiliations they seem to unite and take a common stand on the floor of the House on women specific issues. Some of them also expressed their concern about the indifferent attitude of their male colleagues in the Assembly.

7

SUMMARY AND FINDINGS

7.1 Summary

The last two decades have been marked by critical activities both of women and by women. The growing body of literature and evidence on women's integral involvement in varied structures and processes of society have brought gender to the centrestage of all the developmental efforts. "It is now widely recognized that seemingly well worked out plans and programmes being both gender-biased and gender blind can have disastrous consequences for women" (Kumari, 1994: 33). Efforts are, therefore, being made to develop alternate strategies and discourses that are both gender-sensitive and gender just.

The studies attempted so far on the participation of women in politics are mainly confined to their voting behaviour or at the best partaking of position as candidates, member of legislatures and ministers. The present study has focused on women legislators in UP Assembly to study their participation in political process, particularly to see their socio-economic conditions, their role as leader, the issues they raised in the Assembly and the problems they face being as women politicians.

The question of women's participation in political process and decision-making bodies forms a key concern of the women's movement in India. An analysis of the democratic system and representation of various sections of the population therein reveals that women are far behind. Any assessment of political participation of women in a state like Uttar Pradesh has to start by asking the questions like whether such participation has helped in bringing about or moving towards improvement of the equalities of life of women or whether it simply makes life more livable for women. Whether such participation by women either as individuals or as a group has meant working out alternate strategies for development as well as structure of power. Whether the political intentions which women seek to make start with women as points of departure or merely help women infiltrate systematically in the existing hierarchies of power.

Many studies reveal that the women politicians face peculiar problems in their political life, which are totally unknown to their male counterparts. These inhibit their performance in the Legislative Assembly. "The reasons for women's diminished role in political arena include traditions, physiology, lack of vertical mobility, concern for home and family, psychology and lack of patronage, particularly from senior women politicians" (Bhatt, 1995: 90). There may be many more reasons, which hinder women's active involve-ment in politics. In fact, studies on such issues have been very rare and no systematic and comprehensive study appears to have been done on this issue.

It is, indeed, this that necessitates an analysis of issues that are responsible for limiting women's participation in the political process. Thus, the present study has made an attempt to analyse the background, role and involvement of women in politics and the constraints thereof, if any. The study has been undertaken on the women legislators of Uttar Pradesh Assembly.

7.2 The Statement of Problem — Research Questions

The present study focuses on the following specific questions:

1. Who are the women leaders in UP?
2. How have they emerged as leaders?
3. What role do they play?
4. What kind of issues do they raise in the Assembly? and
5. Whether their social and cultural barriers have stood in their way to participate in politics.

In the first question "who are the women leaders in UP?" we have studied the socio-economic, educational and other background factors of women legislators in the state. Leaders operationally in this study means the elected women legislators to UP Assembly.

There are many other leaders through positional approach like Member of Parliament (MP), Member of Legislative Council (MLA), Municipal Committee Members, Block Samiti Members, Village Panchyat Sarpanch, etc. The present study has been limited to understand the background of the women legislators, in terms of caste, marital status, age, nature of family, occupation and education.

The second question has taken note of the process through which they have emerged as leaders. This indicates the contributing factors and the process through which women legislators have achieved their position of leadership. The process means whether through election, selection and nomination or by any other means they have reached to a position recognized as leader and this also includes their earlier channels of participation. Contributing factors include previous participation in socio-political activities, socialization, chance factors, situation which forces them to get involved in some struggle, or any other political training and participation. All these factors have been studied with reference to those women legislators who were identified as respondents.

The third question, which has been studied, is "what role do they play?" actually means their performance in public life. As leaders, they have to play some roles, which are different from the role of common women. By virtue of occupying a position, i.e. status of a leader at certain level what has been their contribution in the upliftment and empowerment of the women in particular and society in general. This has also involved their role for the welfare and upliftment of their community people, youths and indirectly strengthening the position and support of other male leaders.

This question has also been searching answer for the role of women legislators in their party organizations and forums, the level at which their participation is enabled, the share of responsibilities and leadership roles women are allowed to wield at different elections, their role in managing and conducting campaigns, the opportunities they get to articulate, express and integrate their views and opinion into the party functioning and policy formulations.

The fourth question was related to their performance in the

Assembly. This has to examine the range and depth of women's participation and their involvement in the Assembly proceedings, particularly in raising issues, moving resolutions, debate on Bills, proposing motions, etc. This question has also involved an analysis of 'women' as a group in the Assembly, the occasions and issues on which they cut across party lines and join hands together.

And fifth question was meant to examine the hindrance mainly due to social and cultural barriers that the legislators faced while entering into active politics and performing their role as leader. Some of the major issues, which either facilitate or limit women's participation in the political process, have also been examined in this question.

7.3 Area of Study

The study has been confined to the state of Uttar Pradesh. Uttar Pradesh (UP) politically is a very sensitive and important state in terms of providing leadership. UP, which is socially more backward than many other states in the country, has sent more women into the Central and State legislatures. It has the largest Legislative Assembly, sends largest number of MP in the Parliament and politically has always dominated on the national scene. UP have 80 seats of MPs in the Lok Sabha and 404 seats in the state legislative Assembly. The important leaders have always focused attention on this state. The state of UP has produced many men and women leaders of national and international repute. In fact, the first woman Prime Minister of India belonged to UP. Out of thirteen Prime Ministers of India elected so far, eight were from Uttar Pradesh. More women members of the UP had become members in the Central Cabinet than women from any other state. Both formal and informal leadership can be observed in this state. That is why UP has been selected for the present study. UP has the highest population in the country. The state provides a specific situation by its location, general reputation, social composition, large women voters, socio-cultural history and important centre of political activities. The demographic and other important salient features of UP, position of women in state, their political activities and organisations and political parties they belong to have already been explained in the earlier chapters.

7.4 Identification and Selection of Respondents — Universe and Sample

The UP Legislature consists of the Governor and the two houses known as the legislative Council and the Legislative Assembly. At present, the Legislative Council of UP has 100 members and Legislative Assembly is 404 excluding one member of Anglo-Indian community. The prime unit of our analysis was women legislators in UP Assembly. The women leaders, in the context of our study, consist of all women legislators elected in fourteen Assembly elections held in UP so far, and therefore, constitutes the universe of the present study. A profile of all women legislators including all former women legislators in UP Assembly was prepared and it was observed that about fifty-six women were elected as legislators more than once. Many of them represented continuously their constituencies several times, and some as many as seven times. Although, concerns are specific to women legislators, their male colleagues formed an integral part of our analysis and, therefore, a controlled group of male legislators was to constitute the second unit category of our analysis. But limiting the volume this has been dealt with only illustratively. The study has tried to find out the attitude of her male colleagues toward her and also identify various interventions that can ensure and enhance an increased and qualitatively better participation of women both in Assembly and in political party. Therefore, some male legislators have also been included to form a small part of respondents.

The first Assembly elections in UP, were held in the year 1952 after independence wherein eleven women legislators were elected to the Assembly. The last Assembly election in UP was held in 2002 and 26 women were elected. However, in 1996 elections two had resigned on some pretext or the other and the strength of women legislators was reduced to eighteen only. Since 1952, 14 Assembly elections have been conducted in UP in which a total of 255 women were elected. Out of the total 255 women legislators, 56 women legislators were elected more than once. A list was prepared of all women legislators and it was observed that 56 women have been repeatedly appearing at 166 places in the list. If 56 are excluded from 166, the remaining 110 have to be deducted from the 255 and thus, the total numbers of women legislators were reduced to 145. Out of these 145 legislators, 7 legislators have expired and 12 could not reply queries properly due to their poor health and old age. Fifteen women legislators have not sent filled in questionnaires even after repeated reminders and great persuasion sixteen have been elected first time in 2002 elections. There was no information available about them regarding their age, education, family background, income, profession, etc. in the literature like *Who's Who* published by the Vidhan Sabha secretariat. Thus, there were legislators those who have been expired, other those who could not be contacted and some those who could not answer the queries due to having old age related diseases; such few have been deleted as the case of "sample mortality". Their number is about 50 thus leaving the total respondents as 95.

7.5 Data Collection

All the available and accessible sources were fully explored to collect required information and data on all 95 women legislators in three different stages.

At the initial stage, a comprehensive and in-depth analysis of the existing literature on the political processes and decision-making bodies in particular was made. In the second stage, a structured questionnaire was formulated to extract information from women legislators on specific areas and issues. The questionnaire was designed to obtain facts on personal attributes, information on involvement in politics, association with political party/parties, involvement in electoral politics, role in legislature politics and proceedings, role as a minister, response to certain general and women specific issues, suggestions on an increased and qualitatively better participation of women in political process and decision making bodies.

The questionnaires formulated were then sent to them.

However, only three women legislators sent written responses in the first round.

As only three women legislators sent back the first round of questionnaires (although majority of them confirmed having received them) another round of questionnaires were sent. After persistent reminders only 40 women legislators responded with filled in questionnaires.

Simultaneously, in the third stage, efforts were also made to contact them in person. Personal interviews were held with 40 women legislators (15 sitting and 25 ex-legislators). Most of the sitting women legislators were contacted in Lucknow when Assembly session was on while ex-women legislators (25) were contacted at their residences. Interestingly, they were found to be courteous and cooperative than sitting members.

Case studies of seven women legislators were done. They were selected taking into account the representation of different castes, different leadership positions, their experience and background. One of the important criteria for selection of the case studies was their experience as legislators, the number of times they had represented their constituencies and their position as minister. Legislators belonging to the scheduled castes and OBCs and the legislators from the different parts of the state have been considered to take up the case studies. For describing the case studies, interviews of the legislators, observations, supplementary information through knowledgeable persons and available in their life history in various records have been used. With the co-operation of the legislators as also by our own perceptions and preparations, it could be possible to collect required information on all 95 respondents.

7.6 Data Analysis

The information furnished by the respondents and collected from various other sources was transferred from the notes, diaries, and the interviews schedules to the data sheets and then were analyzed. The huge data on various aspects have been analyzed and arranged in tables for interpretation. The data were analyzed by computing chi-square and co-relational statistics. Case materials, however, were qualitatively analyzed. The information on background variables was quantitatively analyzed. The relationship of various factors has been indicated on the basis of numerical distribution presented in the tables. Thus, the data of 95 respondents have been analyzed using both quantitative and qualitative methods.

7.7 Concepts/Terms

We have used the following concepts as technical terms and tools for precision and abstraction.

7.7.1 *Politics and Political Participation*

"Politics refers to the functioning of a whole array of public institutions and forces which are involved in moulding the lives of people by way of decisions and policies that impinge upon their relations with one another" (Kaushik, 1996: 35). 'Politics' is often defined in very narrow terms as the electoral participation in democracy. The varied activities that are performed by a person in an elected position or as part of the voter's duty, defined as political participation. This is because such participation is expected to be the springboard of decision making in the public sphere that, in turn, is denoted as power.

"The concept of politics has, by and large, been defined either in terms of process or in terms of the peace or place where it happens, i.e. in terms of the 'arena' or the institutional forms (i.e. parliament, assemblies, etc.)" (Kumari: 1996 : 34). However, there does exist an overlapping between the two. Thus, for instance, those who subscribe to the 'arena' concept may regard it as a process but confine this process of politics to certain kind of institutions and organizations. Broadly defined politics refers to a whole gamut of structures and forces that affect people's lives by way of decisions and policies. It involves not merely the availability of opportunities, rights, liberties and justice to both individuals and the groups but also the extent to which they are availed of and exercised.

7.7.2 *Leader*

'Leader' literally means a person who leads or has the capacity to lead. He/she can understand the complexities of the social structures, which are the base of politics, education, economy and social status.

Leader, operationally, defined as one who occupies power position in any organization or association in the government or otherwise. *In the present study, the women legislators who occupy position in the most important decision making body, at the state level, namely, the state Legislature have been considered as the women leaders.*

7.7.3 *Elite*

Several authors have given the concept beginning with Pareto and others. Elite is used in respect of "those positions in a social structures which are supper-ordinate such that the incumbent claims and are granted social superiority". The term is also used to refer to the functions attached to such positions, especially the special responsibility to form and define value standard in a certain social sphere. The leaders defined above consist of 'elites' in political arena of UP.

7.7.4 *Development*

Development is here used to mean both the improved material well being (welfare) of people and the process by which this improved well being is achieved. The concept of development also includes an element of equality — that material benefits from the development process should be fairly distributed, especially benefit to those most in need, the disadvantaged and the most vulnerable. Therefore, the special interest in women's development arises because women are a majority amongst the most disadvantaged.

7.7.5 *Empowerment*

Empowerment is an important element of development, being the process by which people take control and action in order to overcome obstacles. Empowerment especially means the collective action by the oppressed and deprived to overcome the obstacles of structural inequality which have previously put them in a disadvantaged position. It is the process by which women mobilise to understand, identify and overcome gender discrimination, so as to achieve equality of welfare and equal access to resources. Empowerment may be analytically distinguished from "self-reliance"; which may be defined as people's ability to advance themselves within the existing social system.

7.7.6 *Gender Discrimination*

Gender discrimination means to give differential treatment to individuals on the grounds of their gender. In a patriarchal society, this involves systematic and structural discrimination against women in the distribution of income, access to resources, and participation in decision-making.

7.7.7 *Gender Equality*

Gender equality means that there is no discrimination on grounds of a person's sex in the allocation of resources or benefits, or in the access to services. Gender equality may be measured in terms of whether there is equality of opportunity, or equality of results.

7.7.8 *Gender Equity*

It means fairness and justice in the distribution of benefits and responsibilities between the two genders. Gender equality does not have such a well-defined meaning as gender equity, because it's meaning depends on the definition of fairness and justice. In addition, in its legal sense the term equity suggests a limited notion of the concept of justice, since equity refers to justice within the existing law, rather than justice by changing the law.

7.8 Findings

In the present work, it was proposed to study mainly five questions.

These questions were referred to the socio-economic background of the women legislators, their role and performance as leaders, their emergence as leaders, i.e. contributory factors and the process through which they have emerged as leaders, the kind of issues they raised in the Assembly and problems/obstacles (if any) they have faced while entering the politics. These questions have been studied in the context of women legislators of UP Assembly. Ninety-five women legislators were identified in 14 Assembly elections till 2002.

Out of the 95 women legislators, 56 are those who have represented their constituencies more than once and some of them as many as seven times.

On the basis of the facts collected about the 95 women legislators and the seven strategically case studies, the findings on the main questions are presented below:

7.8.1 *Background of the Women Legislators*

(i) Out of the 95 women legislators, 58 are from the General category, 24 are from Scheduled Castes (SCs) and 13 from Other Backward Castes (OBCs). Mostly, the SC women (about 85%) belonged to the Chamar/Jatav and Passi castes. This shows that Chamars/Jatavas and Passies are more developed among SCs than the other 58 remaining castes. In fact, this may be due to the fact that the population of Chamars and Jatavas in the state has been much higher than the other castes falling under SC category. However, there has been no woman legislator from the ST category in the state of UP.

(ii) Age profile of women legislators reveals that the maximum women legislators, about 43 per cent, entered into the Assembly between the age of 30-39 years. A comparative study of age profile of women legislators also reveals that the thirteenth and twelfth Assemblies have the highest representation of women belonging to the age group of 25-30 years. This indicates that more young women have been entering politics presently than in the past. The youngest woman legislator is 25 years of age in the Assembly.

There were only three women legislators in the Assembly above the age of 61 years who joined politics after their retirement from the government service. There were other three women legislators (3.15%) in the age group of 56-60 years. Thus, bulk of the women legislators, forty-three (43.16%) was in the middle age group of 30-39 years. It is little surprising since women of this age bracket are not fairly free from the domestic and family responsibilities.

(iii) Out of 95 women legislators, only 6 were unmarried and 27 were widows at the time of their entry into the politics. Thus, majority (89) of women were married when they entered into the Assembly and, therefore, the marital status "married" appears to be relevant and necessary for all the women leaders.

(iv) The majority of women (53.6%) got married below the age of 17 years. In fact, four legislators were married as a child between the age of 8-11 years, which is much below the prescribed norms. The 16 women legislators who were married as children belonged to the different castes, family background and educational levels (6 from SCs, 4 from OBCs and 6 from general caste). It, therefore, may be said that the child marriage was common among all the castes and in all the parts of UP. Thus, the fact that marriage, *ipso facto* is a hindrance to pursue a political or any other career, stands refuted.

(v) It was found that marital status, age at marriage and the family size of women legislators have not created any direct hindrance in pursuing their political carrier, however, their capacity to participate in politics, to some extent, is related to their marital status and also on the relief she can get from the burden of bearing and rearing of children. Therefore, it may be said that though the factors like marital status, age at marriage and size of family to some extent determines the capacity, efficiency and effectiveness of women legislators in their public participation, but these factors have no direct bearings on their political ambitions.

(vi) Educationally, it was found that women leaders have a variation from being illiterate to higher education. The numbers of graduates and post-graduates are the highest, more than half (52.63 per cent). In the case of undergraduates (33.70 per cent), the position is far better than non-matriculates. The women legislators with doctoral degrees were indeed only two. However, the number of graduates with professional degrees is significant about 18 per cent. Thus women teachers and lawyers were increasingly joining politics than other professionals. Comparative analysis over the years shows that there is a better representation of women having higher level of education in the present Assembly than in the past.

(vii) The undergraduates are also significant in number, about 33.70 per cent and under-matriculates are only 13.68 per cent. This shows that lower or higher education does not appear to be very necessary for entering into the politics. Being an illiterate is also no bar for becoming leaders as a small fraction of women legislators are just literate. However, those who could not complete their graduation (undergraduates), many of them seem to be turning to the politics.

(viii) The education level of women legislators from SC category is equally higher as of the other (General and OBC) castes. In fact, out of 24 women belonging to SC category in the sample, 10 women (41.66%) are graduates and postgraduates and equal numbers are undergraduates. Only four women legislators (16.66%) are under matriculate.

(ix) The family size and caste factors do not seem to be related to their level of education as it could be expected. There are 20 women legislators (21.05%) those are graduates and postgraduates and having 4 to 6 children. They belonged to the different castes. However, out of 4 legislators having more than six children, 3 belonged to the SC category.

(x) The women legislators have come from various occupational groups. A substantial percentage accounting for about 58 have come from agriculture occupation. Next to agriculture, politics and social work have been the occupation of 28% women legislators. The other significant professions are teaching and lawyer, which have significant (18%) representation.

7.8.2 *Emergence of Women Legislators as Leaders*

(xi) Most of the women leaders in the present study belonged to the national political parties like Congress, Samajwadi Party (SP) and Bharatiya Janata Party (BJP). These parties have been in power at one time or the other in the state of UP and most of them even at the Centre as well. Thus, the broader understanding and linkages are in tune with the ideals of the senior party leaders and the emergence of women leadership, therefore, appears to have depended upon the party high command. The high command often made the choices of women candidates for nominating them to contest the elections. Therefore, the emergence of state level leadership is also a show off of the loyalty either to the past or the present leadership of the party high command.

(xii) Majority of women legislators who are seen to be actively engaged in politics have had someone from amongst her close relations in politics. Many women from the grassroots level are also coming up to the Legislature. It is, therefore, pertinent to the question if large-scale participation of women in active politics really exists to elect their representatives to the legislative Assembly.

(xiii) Out of 95 women legislators in the present study, 48 women legislators, about 50 per cent, were having strong family linkages that helped them to become leaders. They have come from the families where the father, brother and mother or husband was in active politics. In those cases, where women legislators came from what may be termed as political families, the familiar opposition/resistance to women entering politics is almost non-existent.

(xiv) The factor that shows the significance of the background of their political career is their family linkages. The interest and understanding acquired through father, brother, husband and such other relations constitute the familial influence for women activists. In the sample, about 30 women legislators (31.58 per cent) were married to persons who were political activists. Though they were elected in their individual capacities, their role was primarily supportive to their husbands who had leading positions in the politics of their respective areas.

(xv) The inter-relationships of above variables have shown that widow succession has been very pervasive in the UP politics. Out of 27 widows in the sample, as many as 20 (74%) were those who had been given tickets after the death of their husbands to fill in void. The widow succession has been without any other considerations than the husband's death and, therefore, no relationship does exist between their education, caste, family background and their emergence as leaders.

(xvi) The association between higher social status and higher rate of participation is also established. Only in the case of women activists with family linkages, this view may be slightly modified because linkage, irrespective of education, is a powerful factor in a woman's politicization and in practical politics.

7.8.3 *Role of Women Legislators*

(xvii) The women leaders have been playing a key role of linkages between the state and the people. Most of the general developmental works like water supply, schools, roads, electricity arrangements, etc. and also the various higher-level official works have easily been completed under the influence of the women legislators. Almost all the women legislators have been able to provide such general facilities for the society as a whole during their terms. The few women legislators could also get the developmental work done at large scale due to their position as ministers. Though, there have been only one or two such women legislators at a time.

(xviii) The role of scheduled caste women legislators for their own caste people has been in the form of social emulsion. Almost all of them have been demanding for the social justice in the legislature, at least for their own caste people. However, a joint action has never been seen in such cases. Their action is guided by the concerned party high command. Even if there is clear-cut case of social injustice, they do not dare to raise their voices against their party high command. Of course, they have sometimes proved to be as a mediator, to disperse the matter, between the government and the victims.

(xix) Another important role, which the scheduled caste women legislators seem to play is that they have been helping their community to get grants from the various governmental agencies for the development of infrastructure in their constituencies and for the social welfare activities.

(xx) Majority of the women legislators, fifty-five (about 58%), have been working directly or indirectly for voluntary social organizations, which are engaged in the welfare activities and working for improving the living conditions of poor and oppressed class. They have been imparting training and education among them, which is ultimately increasing their house hold incomes. Some of them have been working for the rights and the welfare of SCs and STs, industrial workers and the government employees.

(xxi) It was also found that a segment of women legislators has been actively engaged in enhancing the education and residential facilities, self-employment, religious reforms, housing problems, water and sanitation problems, welfare activities for women, girls, poor, widows and persons belonging to the SCs and STs. Besides, they have been working for the eradication of the social evils like dowry, illiteracy and child marriage.

(xxii) Within the parties, there is a marked non-involvement of women in decision-making bodies. In Janata Dal, there is no woman member in Political Affairs Committee. The situation in the Left parties is in no way better than that of Janata Dal. The Congress and BJP members, however, did claim of active involvement of women legislators in the decision making within the party.

(xxiii) As regards the choice of candidates during election, the candidates are generally decided by the male members and are passed on to the women members for ratification, though there are some exceptions. Female members are trusted with such responsibilities as launching an election campaign, holding meetings, etc.

(xxiv) Even in the absence of political or decision making power within the parties, women are not cutting across party lines and uniting on issues like violence and atrocities inflicted on women. The question of solidarity of women on the issue of political power is sidetracked in almost all conversations.

(xxv) Women members were not prone to frequent defections, with a few exceptions. Majority of them have stayed with their original party. In the present study only two cases have been observed wherein women break away and switched over to another party.

7.8.4 *Women Participation in the Assembly Proceedings and Issues Raised*

(xxvi) The participation of women legislators in Assembly proceedings is not so much determined by the gender factor as it is by their numbers. Both men and women legislators are governed by certain set of rules and procedures. However, owing to their small numerical strength, women are in a disadvantaged position.

(xxvii) Moreover, the issue of participation acquires significance in the context of the coming in of the visual media to the House, visibility not in terms of being effective but to be effective. This is as true of women as men.

(xxviii) In the Assembly, women legislators, by and large, cut across party lines and are united on issues relating to violence and atrocities committed against women. On other general issues, they often toe their party line. Sometimes, this is the case even when the issue is of violence or atrocity against a woman, but has happened in the constituencies of incumbent ministers or Chief Minister, the women members from the ruling party take a stand more on party lines than by treating them as women's issues.

(xxix) Women members are given a chance to speak on a variety of issues, which is determined by their respective parties depending on their interest and specialization. They do raise issues apart from women specific problems. The incidence and frequency of raising issues, moving resolutions and initiating discussions is, however, linked both to the experiences of the woman member in terms of time as also her exposure to political activities from grassroots level.

(xxx) When women specific issues are raised, the attendance or non-attendance in Assembly is determined more by the 'time', i.e. prelunch or post-lunch that is being allotted in the agenda of the day's proceedings. Generally, the attendance is relatively thin in the post-lunch session and any issue which is being taken up in the post-lunch session is not well attended unless it is something 'sensational' or has already attracted the nation's attention.

(xxxi) Approximately all the respondents agreed to the suggestion of having time slots for women in a day's agenda during each session both in terms of women members raising any issue as well as any member raising women specific issues. Within the parties, women's issues are categorized as social and not political issues to be dealt exclusively by women's wing.

(xxxii) Generally, it is observed that the party to which the woman belongs to determines the response of women legislators. The fact that women legislators of one political party were quite vociferous in expressing their discontent with their party can be traced to the structure and age of the party itself. An infant party (in terms of political parlance) has structural and organizational problems.

7.8.5 *Problems Faced by the Women Legislators*

(xxxiii) Except one or two legislators, all have denied any difficulty or resistance to their entry in politics. During the course of interview held with them, two legislators, however, categorically said that their children initially were not happy and had objections to their entry in politics. Some of them have faced mild problems and also were manhandled during election campaigns and other visits to their constituencies, as they have narrated some instances of violence inflicted on them during the interview.

(xxxiv) There were few instances where women legislators clearly pointed out that their children were reluctant and were not allowing them to join political life. One woman legislator entered in politics even after a gap of 21 years, though she had sustained her interest all along. There were many other instances where women were born into political families but could join politics only in their 30s and 40s, since they have to pursue their family duties.

(xxxv) Majority of them have to bear the double burden of carrying on their familial responsibilities as well as carrying out their political career.

(xxxvi) On the issue of financial constraints during elections women were not very forthright. They often responded by saying "Kisi Tarah se ho hi jata hai' (it gets arranged somehow).

The analysis of above facts indicates that, by and large, women are treated well on the floor of the House and to quote a male legislator 'women have sobering effect on their male colleagues'. Thus, it may be concluded that most of the women legislators have not faced any difficulty in entering politics. Although one or two have confirmed the initial mild resistance from their family, particularly from their children, but majority of women legislators have denied any hindrance from family or otherwise to their entry into the politics and pursuing their political career further. On the face of it, it appears that women legislators faced no hindrance of any kind at the time of their entry into politics.

The case studies also indicate that the majority of women legislators have come from middle class family and significant number of legislators have family political history and linkages. The general educational level among legislators has improved in comparison to their old counterparts. The women legislators have been playing multi-facet role for the benefit of their own society and public at large. The SC leaders have been playing the role of emulsion of their society and extracting grants from governments for their welfare activities. The participation in the Assembly, more or less, is the function of their numerical strength. The women leaders have denied any hindrance in the entry to their political career.

7.9 Bearing on and the Examination of Concepts/Terms

The meaning of a leader is "one who leads" the other people, groups or a community and expected to bind the community together in achieving the collective goal of social welfare. The findings of the present study suggest that the majority of the women legislators appear to lead local groups of their own castes in particular and other social gatherings in general. The expectation of binding a community does not appear conclusive, however, they have been helping the community for achieving the common goals of the welfare. The women leaders, belonging to SC category, appear excelling in the political activity and advanced to serve as a guide to their own caste people. They have role in setting up the objectives of community welfare, facilitate, manipulation of means and impress upon the instrument of state action for implementation of various welfare policies and programmes for their community people. Majority of them seem to be 'ideal typical' leaders as conceptually characterised. Similarly, the women legislators from the general category have better presence felt as leader in their own society and public at large.

The elites are the people who have higher status/scores in the walk of life. They are superiors having power, organisation, influence and are held in high esteem by the people. In the present study, women leaders have leadership position at various levels in political structure and involuntary organisations. Majority of them are considered to be of high status in general social life. A few are considered superiors and have power to influence the decision making bodies and also have organisation to exercise power. These few would qualify to be held in high esteem by the people at large, but also by their own caste community people. Thus, a majority of women legislators in the present study would be said to be the elites of the society.

As incumbent of leadership position, the women legislators are expected to perform certain activities (roles) and to show a pattern of behaviour expected from them by virtue of occupying leadership position. It has been found that the women leaders have been largely working for the cause of their respective caste people. They accelerate the flow of grants, aid and various benefits from the state for their community's welfare. The women leaders are also channelising the state assistance through various organisations and helping their brethren to fight against atrocities and social discrimination by the other groups. It is thus implied that although the women leaders have been fulfilling expectations of the society to a limited extent, but this pattern of the behaviour is not expected by the society. Their own community people have perceptions that women leaders have not been fulfilling expectations of neither of their brethren nor of the society but only acting as handpicked tools of the few rich and powerful people of the society. Thus, the ideal role performance of women legislators is limited as is expected of incumbents of that position.

Many women leaders appear to exercise influence but largely

in their own community more so at the local level. Society at large feels least influenced and that too by few women leaders only. Therefore, only few women leaders from the high position in the political structure of society have greater influence on the people. Majority of them have limited influence on their local community. Thus it may be said that the majority of women leaders fall in the category of local influentials. A small segment of them have larger area of influence on the wider society and thinks of the outside world of their local area as well and this segment is to be considered as cosmopolitan influentials.

Those groups and individuals from whom the women legislators get inspiration in the process of becoming leaders, performing leadership roles and maintaining leadership positions have been known as their reference groups. In the present study, a large number considers the popular leaders of their own caste/area as their role models. A significant number of women leaders, as the findings suggest, consider Mahatma Gandhi, Pt. Jawaharlal Nehru, Jayaprakash Narayan and Indira Gandhi as their role models to draw inspiration and to lead their community. In the case of women leaders from SC category, majority of them consider Dr. Ambedkar as their role model.

The majority of women legislators agreed to that women are not taken seriously on the floor of the House and, therefore, they appear to be well aware of the gender discrimination. However, their lower participation in the Assembly proceedings is not due to any gender discrimination but mainly due to their lower numerical strength in the Assembly. The gender equality and gender equity seem to be almost non-existent in the party functioning as many important responsibilities in parties are not given to them because of their gender. The women are considered weak and vulnerable to physical assaults and, therefore, generally not allowed to go alone in the election campaign in odd hours in their constituencies.

7.10 Bearing on the Earlier Findings

Some studies, e.g. Bhatt (1995), Seth (1979) have indicated that the majority of the women leaders (MPs) belonged to the economically well-off families and a large segment of them belonged to the higher middle class families. Bhatt study observed that women MP from general constituency had higher educational qualifications as compared to those elected from reserved constituencies. The present study also indicates that majority of women legislators belong to higher middle class family. However, a significant proportion has also come from rural background and lower middle class families. The women legislators from reserved constituencies have better or equal educational qualifications than the legislators from general category. This is contrary to what Bhatt has observed in her studies. Parvathamma (1969) has also indicated that SC elites emerged from the better educational and middle categories and from the upper age group of 41-60 years. The findings of the present study are the same except that the larger group of legislators belongs to the age group of 30-39 years. Kumari and Dubey (1994) studied socio-economic conditions and other related issues like role of women MPs in Parliament proceedings, their association with political parties, the hindrance faced by them and their involvement in electoral politics. They found that many women MPs belonged to families having political background and with support of their parents or spouses; they had established themselves in the organisation or party. Similar trend has been found in the present study as about 43 per cent of the sample have political family background/linkages and 74 per cent widows were those who had been given tickets after the death of their husbands to fill in void. Bhatt (1995) has also indicated the similar finding. Thus the earlier trends get confined that the women leaders are drawn from middle categories and majority of them have political linkages. A larger segment of women legislators appears to have the higher level of education among both SC and general categories. A very small segment, almost negligible, of women leaders is still remained illiterate. SC women leaders are drawn from various castes and among them the majority is from single caste, 'Chamar' / 'Jatav'. But the caste-wise distribution of the leaders corresponds almost directly to the proportion in the total population of SCs. Thus, they appear to be representing their respective castes. Raj Bala (1997) has made similar observation in Haryana.

Important roles of elites in transforming the society was visualised in general in developing countries like India (Bottomore, 1964), and of the SC elites in particular (Sachchidanand, 1974). The present study shows that women legislators are largely bringing in the facilities extended by the state for their societies by acting as linkages and facilitator. They are focusing on the education of the future generation through various voluntary organisations. However, it depends largely on the channelisation of resources from the state which are entirely again depended upon the capability, capacity, experience, influence of women legislators.

The functions of a leader to lead and attract the followers to create unity among the masses have also been examined. A leader is expected to perform four main functions, i.e. (a) the determination of objectives, (b) manipulation of existing means, (c) control of instrument of action, and (d) stimulation of coordinated action. In India, caste is variable in executing any of these functions, particularly in case of SCs. Sachchidanand (1974) also pointed out that the SC elites were not effective in performing the general function of a leader. The above characteristics have not been observed in the present study; rather it is reversed. The majority of women legislators are seen performing their role as leader and they are very effective in their functioning. This has been found among leaders of both the SCs and general categories. The BSP factor seems to be brought a tremendous confidence among women leaders belonging to SC category in UP. A few of them have able to manipulate the existing means of state political power, and have control over the instrumentalities of actions.

The earlier studies done by Bhatt, Kumari, Kaushik and Seth regarding the participation of women politicians in the Parliamentary proceedings and debates on Bills have found that women parliamentarians have very low participation. Bhatt has indicated that this is due mainly to their low numerical strength. In the present study, it is found that the participation of women legislators in Assembly proceedings, particularly in the debates on various Bills and resolutions, has been very low. However, it was also mainly due to their low numerical strength and not because of any gender discrimination. All the male and female legislators are governed by the certain set of rules and procedures to participate in the Assembly debates. Women are at disadvantageous position due to their lower number.

Regarding the issues, women legislators have been raising a variety of general issues and not specific to the women cause. Kumari and Bhatt have made similar observations. While Kumari in her study found that women faced social and cultural barriers while entering the politics, but in the present study, no such indication has emerged as almost all the women legislators have denied any hindrance of social or cultural type while entering the active politics.

7.11 Problems and Limitations of the Present Study

Arranging the timings for meeting with women legislators for their interview proved to be an extremely challenging and arduous task 'in terms of their availability and also willingness to co-operate. Persistent and continuous efforts, therefore, had to be made to contact them. With the selected sitting women legislators, personal interviews were held. This did not prove to be an easy job. The written response from them to filled in questionnaires has also not been encouraging. However, presumably due to the paucity of time owing to a hectic schedule, only a few women legislators sent written responses in the first round. Then many repeated reminders were sent to them and after great persuasions, only 40 women sent reply to the queries.

One of the major constraints of the present study has been the limited availability of the women legislators. It is merely a qualitative exercise that is geared towards generating a debate on the issue of women political participation and intends to raise a number of questions rather than provide answers.

Moreover, as the majority of women legislators expressed their inability to send a written response to our questionnaire, collecting information on specific issues became extremely tardy. This was worsened by the paucity of literature (specifically) on women legislators. Although a vast amount of literature, and one that is constantly growing is readily available on women, no systematic and comprehensive studies have been done on women legislators. The Who's Who available with the Assemblies and Lok Sabha Secretariats may help to draw a biographical profile of women legislators but it does not give such information as how and when the legislators got involved in politics, the problems and constraints faced by her in political career/life etc., which are more crucial for the analysis. Although, the Secretariats have now started segregating information on gender basis, by and large, the available information and documented proceedings are not gender-specific. Further, even this information was not easily accessible.

Even the Vidhan Sabha Secretariats attached to both the Houses of legislature have just begun to segregate and document their information on gender basis. Although this paucity of literature, specifically on women legislators, did make our task difficult to a certain extent, it is in fact provided with a challenging opportunity to explore an area that has hitherto been by and large left untouched.

The present study has taken note of women legislators in the UP Assembly only. This remained limited to analyse their socio-economic, educational background, to some extent, the factors and processes of emergence of leaders, their roles and performance within their positional structure and their participation in Assembly proceedings, the issues they raised and to the exploration of factors and relationships. Another limitation of the present study has been the very poor and unclear response to the queries from the respondents (women legislators). The systematic availability of information on gender basis is also not readily available in the Vidhan Sabha Secretariat and other published literature.

The network of all women leaders in the wider complex and within the local context, therefore, could not be dealt with since the study focused upon the UP Assembly only. There is a need of detailed analysis to depict upon the linkages of women leaders in the local social structure and the wider political structure. The further study may include all women politicians in the state of UP at various levels, i.e. panchayat, district and state together and should draw the comparison and their effectiveness as women leaders with male leaders. Systematic qualification of factors contributing to emergence of leaders, counting effectively their roles and depth and quality of their participation in the Assembly proceedings particularly in debates and discussions remains to be attempted exhaustively.

7.12 Conclusion

(i) Although criminalisation of politics appears to hinder the entry of women into political processes, it was felt that increase in the number of women in the political process and decision-making bodies will help in countering this problem.

(ii) It was opined that an analysis based on the continuous interlinking of categories of 'class' and 'gender' would be more fruitful than treating either of the two exclusively.

(iii) Women must be brought in from the grassroots level and should be given position of power in the decision-making processes.

(iv) There should be an increase in the numerical strength of women at different levels — from lower to higher — the concept of women as a critical mass.

(v) Political training should be imparted to both men and women legislators. There is an urgent need to create a political will to change the attitude of people and process and not merely 'politics as social work'.

(vi) Education plays an important role as far as entry of women legislators into politics is concerned. Women have to be educated so as to bring them into the mainstream of national politics.

(vii) At the level of Assembly, women must not be restricted to the realm of 'party politics', but they must involve themselves with the various committees of the Assembly as well.

(viii) Majority of women legislators have suggested that there should be 30 per cent reservation for women in the Assembly and Parliament. This will not only increase their numbers but also give the opportunity to women to fight the discrimination against them.

APPENDICES

UP Assembly Elections-Elected Women Legislators (2002 - 1952)

Year	*S.No*	*Candidate's Name*	*Constituency*	*Category*	*Party*
2002	1	Ambesh Kumari	Charkhari	SC	SP
2002	2	Amita Singh	Amethi	SC	BJP
2002	3	Anuradha. Chaudhari	Baghra	GEN	RLD
2002	4	Arun Kumari	Bhognipur	GEN	SP
2002	5	Aruna Tornar	Sarsaul	GEN	SP
2002	6	Asha Kishor	Salon	SC	SP
2002	7	Beena Bhardwaj	Bilaspur	SC	SP
2002	8	Fasiha Murad Lari Alias G	Salempur	SC	BSP
2002	9	Geeta Singh	Balrampur	SC	SP
2002	10	Gulab Devi	Chandausi	GEN	BJP
2002	11	Krishna Paswan	Kishunpur	GEN	BJP
2002	12	Luis Khursheed	Kaimganj	SC	INC
2002	13	Mayavati Persad	Srinagar	SC	BSP
2002	14	Mayawati	Jahangirganj	SC	BSP
2002	15	Mayawati	Harora	SC	BSP
2002	16	Omwati Devi	Nagina	GEN	SP
2002	17	Prem Lata Katiyar	Kalyanpur	SC	BJP
2002	18	Raj Laxmi Verma	Ramnagar	SC	BJP
2002	19	Raj Rani	Fatchpur	GEN	BJP
2002	20	Sandhya Katheriya	Kishni	SC	SP
2002	21	Shradha Devi	Mundera Baz	GEN	SP
2002	22	Sukh Devi Verma	Lakhana	SC	SP
2002	23	Uma	Charthawal	SC	BSP
2002	24	Usha Verma	Ahirori	GEN	SP
2002	25	Vidya Chaudhary	Mehnagar	GEN	BSP
2002	26	Vijaya Yadav	Jhusi	GEN	SP
1996	1	Gauri Devi	Kauriram	SC	SP
1996	2	Gulab Devi	Chandausi	SC	BJP
1996	3	Gyanwati Singh	Khair	Sc	BJP
1996	4	Krishna Rawat	Malihabad	GEN	BJP
1996	5	Manju	Ballia	Sc	IND
1996	6	Mayavati Persad	Srinagar	Sc	BSP
1996	7	Mayawati	Bilsi	Sc	BSP
1996	8	Mayawati	Harora	GEN	BSP

Year	*S.No*	*Candidate's Name*	*Constituency*	*Category*	*Party*
1996	9	Mithlesh Kumari	Jalesar	GEN	BJP
1996	10	Omwati Devi	Nagina	GEN	SP -
1996	11	Prabha. Diwedi	Farukhabad	SC	BJP
1996	12	Prem Lata Katiyar	Kalyanpur	GEN	BJP
1996	13	Raja Rai Singh	Pilibhit	GEN	BJP
1996	14	Ram Sakhi	Koil	SC	BJP
1996	15	Seema dwivedi	Garwara	GEN	BJP
1996	16	Subhawati Devi	Maniram	GEN	SP
1996	17	Sukh Devi Verma	Lakhana	GEN	SP
1996	18	Suman Lata Singh	Sunha	SC	BJP
1996	19	Susheela Devi	Muzaffar Nag	GEN	BJP
1996	20	Urmila Devi Yadav	Ghiror	SC	SP
1996	21	Vijaya Yadav	Jhusi	GEN	SP
1993	1	Jadu Rani	Ahirori	SC	SP
1993	2	Jyostana Srivastava	Varanasi Cont	GEN	BJP
1993	3	Prabha Rawat	Sahajanwa	GEN	SP
1993	4	Prem Lata Katiyar	Kalyanpur	GEN	BJP
1993	5	Raj Laxmi Verma	Ram Nagar	SC	BJP
1993	6	Rekha Chhaghal	Ajitmal	GEN	BSP
1993	7	Savitri Devi	Mariahu	GEN	SP
1993	8	Shashi Bala Bharti	Paila	GEN	BJP
1993	9	Shasi Bala Pundir	Deoband	OBC	BJP
1993	10	Sukh Devi Verma	Lakhana	SC	SP
1993	11	Sushila Saroj	Beniganj	SC	BJP
1993	12	Urmila Devi Yadav	Ghiror	GEN	SP
993		13 Urmila Rajput	Kamalganj	SC	BJP
991	1	Gulab Devi	Chandausi	GEN	BJP
991	2	Gyanwati Singh	Iglas	GEN	BJP
991	3	Jyostana Srivastava	Varanasi Cont	GEN	BJP
991	4	Neclam Singh	Mahisi	GEN	BJP
991	5	Padma Seth	Biswan	SC	INC
991	6	Prem Lata Katiyar	Kalyanpur	GEN	BJP
991	7	Sharda Chauhan	Zamania	SC	BJP
991	8	Sharda Devi	Mundera. Baz	GEN	JD
991	9	Urmila Rajput	Kamal Ganj	GEN	BJP
991	10	Vimala Rakesh	Harora	GEN	JD
989	1	Chander Kali Verma	Laharpur	GEN	BJP
989	2	Gauri Devi	Kauriram	OBC	JD
989	3	Kamla Sahani	Shaharat Gar	GEN	INC
989	4	Laljhari Devi	Gauri Bazar	GEN	IND
989	5	Padma Seth	Biswan	OBC	INC
989	6	Premwati	Lucknow(Cant	OBC	INC
989	7	Pushpa Devi	Gannaur	GEN	INC
1989	8	Raj Pati Devi	Gauri Ganj	GEN	INC
1989	9	Rameshwari	Bijnore	GEN	BSP
1989	10	Reshma Arif	Aryanagar	SC	JD
1989	11	Santosh K. Pathak	Data Ganj	SC	BJP

Year	*S.No*	*Candidate's Name*	*Constituency*	*Category*	*Party*
1989	12	Saraswati Tiwari	Almora	GEN	INC
1989	12	Savitri Devi	Madiyahun	GEN	JD
1989	13	Sharda Devi	Munder Bazar	GEN	JD
1989	14	Shashi Mittal	Meerut(Cantt.	SC	BJP
1989	15	Sia Dulari	Manikpur	OBC	INC
1989	16	Sukhda Mishra.	Etawah	SC	JD
1989	17	V. Lakshmi	Bansdoha	GEN	JD
1989	18	Vimala Rakesh	Harora	GEN	JD
1985	1	A. Ammal	Basti	GEN	INC(I)
1985	2	Ashraf Imam	Mirzapur	GEN	INC
1985	3	Beni Bai	Babina	SC	INC
1985	4	Charu Shila	Muzaffar Nag	GEN	INC
1985	5	Genda Devi	Hainsar Bazar	SC	INC(I)
1985	6	H. Kumari	Debai	GEN	INC
1985	7	K. Begum	Sandila	GEN	INC
1985	8	K. Dariyawadi	Sisaman	SC	INC
1985	9	Kamla Sahani	Shonratgarh	GEN	INC(I)
1985	10	Kanti singh Vesien	Lakhimpur	GEN	INC
1985	11	Krishna Rawat	Malihabad	SC	INC
1985	12	Omwati Devi	Nagina	SC	SP
1985	13	P. Singhal	Moradabad	GEN	INC
1985	14	P. Tiwari	Lucknow Cont	GEN	INC
1985	15	Padma Seth	Biswan	GEN	INC
1985	16	Permila Bhadwar	Budaun	GEN	INC
1985	17	Pushpa Devi	Gannaur	GEN	INC
1985	18	Raj Pati Devi	Gauri Ganj	GEN	INC(I)
1985	19	Ram Nandini Verma	Umardha	GEN	LKD
1985	20	Reena Kumary	Kunderki	GEN	INC
1985	21	S. Sharma	Fazil Nagar	GEN	INC
1985	22	S.K. Bakshi	Lucknow (E)	GEN	INC
1985	23	Saraswati Tiwari	Almora	GEN	LKD
1985	24	Saroj Verma	Chaprauli	GEN	LKD
1985	25	Sharda Devi	Mundera Baz	SC	LKD
1985	26	Sukhda Mishra	Etawah	GEN	INC
1985	27	U. Agnihotri	Soron	GEN	INC
1985	28	Uma Tripathi	Hardoi	GEN	INC
1985	29	V. Lakshmi	Bansdih	GEN	JNP
1985	30	Vimala Rakesh	Harora	SC	JNP
1985	31	Vimla Singh	Modinagar	GEN	INC
1980	1	A. Ammal	Basti	GEN	INC(I)
1980	2	Beni Bai	Babina	SC	INC(I)
1980	3	Gauri Devi	Kaurirm	GEN	JNPJP
1980	4	Genda Devi	Hinsari Baza	GEN	INC(I)
1980	5	K. Begum	Sandila	GEN	INC
1980	6	K. Dariyawadi	Sisamau	SC	INC(I)
1980	7	Kamla Devi	Pihani	GEN	INC

Year	*S.No*	*Candidate's Name*	*Constituency*	*Category*	*Party*
1980	8	Kamla. Sahani	Shohrat	GEN	INC(I)
1980	9	Kishori Shukla	Sahjanan	GEN	INC(I)
1980	10	P. Tiwari	Lucknow Cont	GEN	Janata
1980	11	Parwati Devi	Nawab Ganj	GEN	INC
1980	12	Premwati	Gunnaur	GEN	INC
1980	13	Pushpa Chauhan	Sikandranoa	GEN	INC(I)
1980	14	Raj Pati Devi	Gauri Ganj	GEN	INC (I)
1980	15	S.K. Bakshi	Lucknow (E)	GEN	INC
1980	16	S.L. Dikshit	General Gani	GEN	INC
1980	17	Santosh K. Pathak	Data Ganj	GEN	INC(I)
1980	18	Sukhda Mishra	Etawah	GEN	INC
1980	19	Sunita Chauhan	Sareni	GEN	INC(I)
1980	20	Vimala. Rakesh	Harora	SC	JNP
1977	1	Bimla	Harora	SC	JNP
1977	2	K. Begum	Sandila.	GEN	INC
1977	3	M. Sharma	Muzaffar Nag	GEN	JNP
1977	4	Pushpa Devi	Kalyanpur	GEN	JNP
1977	5	R.R. Devi	Jahangiri Gan	SC	JNP
1977	6	S. Nayar	Fakharpur	GEN	INC
1977	7	S. Prabha	Kunda	GEN	JNP
1977	8	S.K. Bakshi	Lucknow (E)	GEN	JNP
1977	9	Sharda Devi	Mundera Baz	GEN	INC
1977	10	Sunita Chauhan	Sareni	SC	JNP
1977	11	Surya Mukhi Sharma	Jhansi	GEN	JNP
1977	12	Uma Tripathi	Hardoi	GEN	INC
1974	1	Beni Bai	Mauranipur	SC	INC
1974	2	Champawati	Fatehpur Sikr	GEN	INC
1974	3	Dulara. Devi	Ikauma	SC	INC
1974	4	Gaytri Devi	Gokul	GEN	BKD
1974	5	Genda Devi	Nagina	GEN	INC
1974	6	Indra Mohini	Kunderki	SC	INC
1974	7	Kailash Pati	Malihabad	SC	INC
1974	8	Mohsina Kidwai	Mausauli	SC	INC
1974	9	Parwati Devi	Nawab Ganj	GEN	JNPSR
1974	10	R.K. Bajpai	Allahabad (N)	GEN	INC
1974	11	R.R. Devi	Jahangiri Gan	SC	INC
1974	12	Raj Pati Devi	GauriGan'	INC	GEN
1974	13	Rama	Almora	GEN	INC
1974	14	S.C. Guriya	Kashimpur	GEN	INC
1974	15	S.K. Bakshi	Lucknow (E)	GEN	INC
1974	16	S.K. Dubey	Birapur	GEN	INC
1974	17	Santosh K. Pathak	Dataganj	GEN	INC
1974	18	Saraswati Devi	Bageshwar	SC	INC
1974	19	Shakuntala	Harora	SC	INC
1974	20	Shyama Devi	Basti	GEN	INC
1974	21	Sukhda Mishra	Etawah	GEN	INC

Year	*S.No*	*Candidate's Name*	*Constituency*	*Category*	*Party*
1974	22	Sunita Chauhan	Rai Barch	GEN	INC
1969	1	Asha Singh	Hardoi	GEN	INC
1969	2	Gaytri Devi	Iglas	GEN	BKD
1969	3	H. Habibullah	Hader Garh	GEN	INC
1969	4	Indra Mohini	Chandausi	GEN	INC
1969	5	K. Begum	Sandila	GEN	INC
1969	6	Kala, Rani	Bilgram.	GEN	INC
1969	7	Manwali Devi	Bikapur	GEN	INC
1969	8	Masali Devi	Bansgaon	GEN	SSP
1969	9	Pyari	Pharanda	GEN	INC
1969	10	R. Kishori	Basti	GEN	INC
1969	11	R.K. Bajpai	Allahabad (N)	GEN	INC
1969	12	Raj Pati Devi	Gauri Ganj	GEN	INC
1969	13	S. Kumari	Data Ganj	SC	INC
1969	14	Saraswati Devi	Bageswar	GEN	INC
1969	15	Shakuntala	Harora	SC	INC
1969	16	Sia Dulari	Manikpur	SC	INC
1969	17	Subhagya: Wati	Aonla	GEN	BKD
1969	18	Vidyawati	Mohammadab	GEN	INC
1967	1	Beni Bai	Mauranipur	GEN	INC
1967	2	Indra Mohini	Chandausi	GEN	INC
1967	3	Jasoda	Dhuriapur	SC	SC
1967	4	Kala Rani	Bilgrama	GEN	INC
1967	5	Masali Devi	Bansgoa	GEN	SSP
1967	6	R.K. Bajpai	Allahabad (N)	GEN	INC
1967	7	Shakuntala.	Harora	SC	INC
1962	1	Beni Bai	Mau	SC	INC
1962	2	Brij Rani Devi	Bithoor	GEN	INC
1962	3	Champawati	Fatehpur	GEN	INC
1962	4	Genda Devi	Khalilabad	SC	INC
1962	5	Jasoda	Dhuriapur	SC	INC
1962	6	Kala Rani	Bilgram	GEN	INC
1962	7	Kishwar Aro	Rampur City	GEN	INC
1962	8	P. Kishori	Basti	GEN	INC
1962	9	Prakash Wati Sood	Meerut Cantt.	GEN	INC
1962	10	R.K. Bajpai	Allahabad Cit	GEN	INC
1962	11	R.R. Devi	Akbarpur	SC	INC
1962	12	S. Nayar	Nagar	GEN	BJS
1962	13	S. Rohatgi	Kanpur CitY	GEN	INC
1962	14	Shakuntala	Sarsawa	SC	INC
1962	15	Shradha Devi	Kithore	GEN	INC
1962	16	Sia Dulari	Manikpur	SC	INC
1962	17	Sucheta Kripalani	Mandhwal	GEN	INC
1962	18	Tara Aggarwal	Kanpur CitY	GEN	INC
1962	19	V. Lakshmi	Deoprayag	GEN	INC
1962	20	Vidyawati	Bah	GEN	INC

Year	S.No	Candidate's Name	Constituency	Category	Party
1957	1	Amola. Devi	Atheha	GEN	INC
1957	2	Beni Bai	Mau	SC	INC
1957	3	Bindumati Devi	Pratab Ganj	GEN	INC
1957	4	Brij Rani Devi	Bilhaur	GEN	INC
1957	5	Chandrawati	Bijnore	SC	INC
1957	6	Dulara Devi	Fakharpur	SC	INC
1957	7	Genda Devi	Khalillabad	SC	INC
1957	8	K.K. Goindi	Karchana	GEN	INC
1957	9	Jasoda	Bansogaon	SC	INC
1957	9	Kailashwati	Chillupar	GEN	INC
1957	10	Prabhawati Devi	Lambhua	GEN	INC
1957	11	Prakash Wati Sood	Meerut Cantt-	GEN	INC
1957	12	R. Kishorf.	Domariaganj (	GEN	INC
1957	13	R.R. Devi	Akabarpur	SC	INC
1957	14	Saijan Devi Manhot	Shoorpur	GEN	JAN
1957	15	Saraswati Devi	Sarju	GEN	INC
1957	16	Satyavati	Dadri	GEN	INC
1957	17	Shakuntala	Harora	SC	INC
1957	18	Shradha Devi	Kithore	GEN	INC
1957	19	Sukhrani	Fatehpur	SC	INC
1957	20	Sunita Chauhan	Salon	GEN	INC
1957	21	Tara Devi	Mariahu	GEN	INC
1957	22	V. Bajpai	Shahabad	GEN	INC
1957	23	V. Lakshmi	Deoprayag	GEN	INC
1952	1	Asha Lata Vyas	Phulpur (Sout	SC	INC
1952	2	Brij Rani Devi	Akbarpur (Bil	GEN	INC
1952	3	Chandrawati	Bijnore Centr	SC	INC
1952	4	Jamuna	Chajipur	GEN	INC
1952	5	Jasoda	Banagaon	SC	INC
1952	6	Laxmi Devi	Sandila.	GEN	RRP
1952	7	Paremeshari Devi	Jaunpur(SOu	GEN	INC
1952	8	Prakash Wati Sood	Hapur North	SC	INC
1952	9	Sajjan Devi Manhot	Gonda (East)	GEN	INC
1952	10	Savitri Devi	Masafirkhanal	GEN	INC
1952	11	Vidyawati	Eatah East	GEN	INC

Source: Report On the General Elections in India 1952 to 2002, Election Commission of India, New Delhi.

LIST OF WOMEN LEGISLATORS ELECTED IN ALL THE FOURTEEN ASSEMBLY ELECTIONS (1952-2002)

U.P Assembly Elections-Elected Women Legislator 2002

S.No	*Candidate's Name*	*Constituency*	*Category*	*Party*
1	Ambesh Kumari	Charkhari	SC	SP
2	Arnita Singh	Amethi	SC	BJP
3	Anuradha Chaud	Baghra	GEN	RLD
4	Arun Kumari	Bhognipur	GEN	SP
5	Aruna Tomar	Sarsaul	GEN	SP
6	Asha Kishor	Salon	SC	SP
7	Beena Bhardwaj	Bilaspur	SC	SP
8	Fasiha. Murad Lar	Salempur	SC	BSP
9	Geeta Singh	Balrampur	SC	SP
10	Gulab Devi	Chandausi	GEN	BJP
11	Krishna Paswan	Kishunpur	GEN	BJP
12	Luis Khursheed	Kaimganj	SC	INC
13	Mayavati Persad	Srinagar	SC	BSP
14	Mayawati	Jahangirganj	SC	BSP
15	Mayawati	Harora	SC	BSP
16	Orawati Devi	Nagina	GEN	SP
17	Prem Lata Katiyar	Kalyanpur	SC	BJP
18	Raj Laxmi Verma	Ramnagar	SC	BJP
19	Raj Rani	Fatehpur	GEN	BJP
20	Sandhya Katheriy	Kishni	SC	SP
21	Shradha Devi	Mundera Bazar	GEN	SP
22	Sukh Devi Verma	Lakhana	SC	SP
23	Uma	Charthawal	SC	BSP
24	Usha Verma	Ahirori	GEN	SP
25	Vidya Chaudhary	Mehnagar	GEN	BSP
26	Vijaya Yadav	Jhusi	GEN	SP

Total Seats = 404

(Note : Mayawati Contested elections from two constituencies and won from both, therefore, actual numbers of women Legislators is 25.)

Source: A Statistical Report On General Elections, 2002 to Lesiglative Assembly of U.P, Election Commission of India, New Delhi.

UP Assembly Elections-Elected Women Legislator 1996

SNo	*Candidate's Name*	*Constituency*	*Category*	*Party*
1	Gauri Devi	Kauriram	SC	SID
2	Gulab Devi	Chandausi	SC	BJP
3	Gyanwati Singh	Khair	SC	BJP
4	Krishna Rawat	Malihabad	GEN	BJP
5	Manju	Ballia	SC	IND
6	Mayavati Persad	Srinagar	SC	BSP
7	Mayawati	Bilsi	SC	BSP
8	Mayawati	Harora	GEN	BSP
9	Mithlesh Kumari	Jalesar	GEN	BJP
10	Omwati Devi	Nagina	GEN	SP
11	Prabha Diwedi	Farukhabad	SC	BJP
12	Prem Lata Katiyar	Kalyanpur	GEN	BJP
13	Raja Rai Singh	Pilibhit	GEN	BJP
14	Ram Sakhi	Koil	SC	BJP
15	Seema dwivedi	Garwara	GEN	BJP
16	Subhawati Devi	Maniram	GEN	SP
17	Sukh Devi Verma	Lakhana	GEN	SP
18	Suman Lata Singh	Sunha	SC	BJP
19	Susheela Devi	Muzaffar Nagar	GEN	BJP
20	Urmila Devi Yadav	Ghiror	SC	SP
21	Vijaya Yadav	Jhusi	GEN	SP

Total Seats = 425

(*Note* : Mayawati was elected from two constituencies and she resigned from both after elected to Lok Sabha. Omwati Devi also resigned and there fore, actual no. of women Legislators were 18.)

Source : Statistical Report On General Election, 1996 to the legislative Assembly of UP Page. 25-33, Election Commission of India, New Delhi.

U.P Assembly El ections-Elected Women Legislator 1993

S.No	*Candidate's Name*	*Constituena*	*Category*	*Party*
1	Jadu Rani	Ahirori	SC	SP
2	Jyostana Srivastava	Varanasi Contt.	GEN	BJP
3	Prabha Rawat	Sahajanwa	GEN	SP
4	Prem Lata Katiyar	Kalyanpur	GEN	BJP
5	Raj Laxmi Verma	Ram Nagar	SC	BJP
6	Rekha Chhaghal	Ajitmal	GEN	BSP
7	Savitri Devi	Mariahu	GEN	SP
8	Shashi Bala Bharti	Paila	GEN	BJP
9	Shasi Bala Pundir	Deoband	OBC	BJP
10	Sukh Devi Verma	Lakhana	SC	SP
11	Sushila Saroj	Beniganj	SC	BJP

S.No	Candidate's Name	Constituency	Category	Party
12	Urmila Devi Yadav	Ghiror	GEN	SP
13	Urmila Rajput	Kaxnalganj	SC	BJP

Total Seats = 425

Source : Report on General Election 1993 to the Legislative Assembly and Bye-election 1993-94 of UP Page 232-244, Election Commission of India, New Delhi. (Figure available in *Who's Who* published by Vidhan Sabha is only 11.

U.P Assembly Elections-Elected Women Legislator 1991

SNo	Candidate's Name	Constituency	Category	Party
1	Gulab Devi	Chandausi	GEN	BJP
2	Gyanwati Singh	Iglas	GEN	BJP
3	Jyostana Srivastava	Varanasi Contt.	GEN	BJP
4	Neelam Singh	Mahisi	GEN	BJP
5	Padrna Seth	Biswan	SC	INC
6	Prem Lata Katiyar	Kalyanpur	GEN	BJP
7	Sharda Chauhan	Zamania	SC	BJP
8	Sharda Devi	Mundera Bazar	GEN	JD
9	Urmila Rajput	Kamal Ganj	GEN	BJP
10	Vimala Rakesh	Harora	GEN	JD

Total Seats = 425

Source : Statistical Report on General Election, 1991 and Bye-election, 1991 to Legslative Assembly of UP. Page: 211-221. Election Commission of India, New Delhi.

U.P Assembly Elections-Elected Women Legislator 1989

SNo	Candidate's Name	Constituency	Category	Party
1	Chander Kali Verma	Laharpur	GEN	BJP
2	Gauri Devi	Kauriram	OBC	JD
3	Kamla Sahani	Shaharat Garh	GEN	INC
4	Laljhari Devi	Gauri Bazar	GEN	IND
5	Padma Seth	Biswan	OBC	INC
6	Premwati	Lucknow(Cantt.)	OBC	INC
7	Pushpa Devi	Gannaur	GEN	INC
8	Raj Pati Devi	Gauri Ganj	GEN	INC
9	Rameshwari	Bijnore	GEN	BSP
10	Reshma Arif	Aryanagar	SC	JD
11	Santosh K. Pathak	Data Ganj	SC	BJP
12	Saraswati Tiwari	Almora.	GEN	INC
13	Savitri Devi	Madiyahun	GEN	JD

S.No	Candidate's Name	Constituency	Category	Party
14	Sharda Devi	Munder Bazar	GEN	JD
15	Shashi Mittal	Meerut(Cantt.)	SC	BJP
16	Sia Dulari	Manikpur	OBC	INC
17	Sukhda Mishra	Etawah	SC	JD
18	V. Lakshmi	Bansdoha	GEN	JD
19	Vimala Rakesh	Harora	GEN	JD

Total Seats = 425

Source: Statistical Report On General Election, 1989 to the Legislative Assembly of U.P. Election Commission of India, New Delhi.

UP Assembly Elections-Elected Women Legislator 1985

SNo	Candidate's Name	Constituency	Category	Party
1	A. Ammal	Basti	GEN	INC(I)
2	Ashraf Imam	Mirzapur	GEN	INC
3	Beni Bai	Babina	SC	INC
4	Charu Shila	Muzaffar Nagar	GEN	INC
5	Genda Devi	Hainsar Bazar	SC	INC(1)
6	H. Kumari	Debai	GEN	INC
7	K. Begum	Sandila	GEN	INC
8	K. Dariyawadi	Sisaman	SC	INC
9	Kamla Sahani	Shonratgarh	GEN	INC(I)
10	Kanti singh Vesien	Lakhimpur	GEN	INC
11	Krishna Rawat	Malihabad	SC	INC
12	Omwati Devi	Nagina	SC	SID
13	P. Singhal	Moradabad	GEN	INC
14	P. Tiwari	Lucknow Contt.	GEN	INC
15	Padma Seth	Biswan	GEN	INC
16	Permila Bhadwar	Budaun	GEN	INC
17	Pushpa Devi	Gannaur	GEN	INC
18	Raj Pati Devi	Gauri Ganj	GEN	INC(I)
19	Ram Nandini Verma	Umardha	GEN	LKD
20	Reena Kumary	Kunderki	GEN	INC
21	S. Sharma	Fazil Nagar	GEN	INC
22	S.K. Bakshi	Lucknow (E)	GEN	INC
23	Saraswati Tiwari	Almora	GEN	LKD
24	Saroj Verma	Chaprauh	GEN	LKD
25	Sharda Devi	Mundera Bazar	SC	LKD
26	Sukhda Mishra	Etawah	GEN	INC
27	U. Agnihotri	Soron	GEN	INC
28	Uma Tripathi	Hardoi	GEN	INC
29	V. Lakshmi	Bansdih	GEN	JNP
30	Vimala Rakesh	Harora	SC	JNP
31	Vimla Singh	Modinagar	GEN	INC

Total Seats = 425

Source : Statistical Report On General Election, 1984-1985 to the Legislative Assembly of UP Page: 664-673, Election Commission of India, New Delhi.

U.P Assembly Elections-Elected Women Legislator 1980

SNo	Candidate's Name	Constituency	Category	Party
1	A. Ararnal	Basti	GEN	INC(I)
2	Beni Bai	Babina	SC	INC(I)
3	Gauri Devi	Kaurirm	GEN	JNPJP
4	Genda Devi	Hinsari Bazar	GEN	INC(I)
5	K. Begurn	Sandila	GEN	INC
6	K. Dariyawadi	Sisamau	SC	INC(I)
7	Kamla Devi	Pihani	GEN	INC
8	Kamla Sahani	Shohrat	GEN	INC(I)
9	Kishori Shulda	Sahjanan	GEN	INC(I)
10	P. Tiwari	Lucknow Contt.	GEN	Janata
11	Parwati Devi	Nawab Ganj	GEN	INC
12	Prernwati	Gunnaur	GEN	INC
13	Pushpa Chauhan	Sikandr~anoa	GEN	INC(I)
14	Raj Pati Devi	Gauri Ganj	GEN	INC (I)
15	S.K. Bakshi	Lucknow (E)	GEN	INC
16	S.L. Dikshit	General Ganj	GEN	INC
17	Santosh K. Patha	Data Ganj	GEN	INC(I)
18	Sukhda Mishra	Etawah	GEN	INC
19	Sunita Chauhan	Sareni	GEN	INC(I)
20	Vimala Rakesh	Harora	SC	JNP

Total seats =425

Source : Statistical Reporl On General Election,1 979-1980 to the Legislative Assembly of U.P. Vol II-A Page: 664-673, Election Commission of India, New Delhi.

U.P Assembly Elections-Elected Women Legislator 1977

SNo	Candidate's Name	Constituency	Category	Party
1	Bimla	Harora	SC	JNP
2	K. Begum	Sandila	GEN	INC
3	M. Sharma	Muzaffar Nagar	GEN	JNP
4	Pushpa Devi	Kalyanpur	GEN	JNP
5	R.R. Devi	Jahangiri Ganj	SC	JNP
6	S. Nayar	Fakharpur	GEN	INC
7	S. Prabha	Kunda	GEN	JNP
8	S.K. Bakshi	Lucknow (E)	GEN	JNP
9	Sharda Devi	Mundera Bazar	GEN	INC
10	Sunita. Chauhan	Sareni	SC	JNP
11	Surya Mukhi Sharma	Jhansi	GEN	JNP
12	Uma. Tripathi	Hardoi	GEN	INC

Total seats = 425

Source : Statistical Report On General Election,1977 to the Legislative Assembly of U.P. Election Commission of India, New Delhi. And Who's Who 1977 published by Vidhan Sabha.

U.P Assembly Elections-Elected Women Legislator 1974

SNo	*Candidate's Name*	*Constituency*	*Category*	*Party*
1	Beni Bai	Mauranipur	SC	INC
2	Champawati	Fatehpur Sikri	GEN	INC
3	Dulara Devi	Ikauma	SC	INC
4	Gaytri Devi	Gokul	GEN	BKD
5	Genda Devi	Nagina	GEN	INC
6	Indra Mohini	Kunderki	SC	INC
7	Kailash Pati	Malihabad	SC	INC
8	Mohsina Kidwai	Mausauli	SC	INC
9	Parwati Devi	Nawab Ganj	GEN	JNPSR
10	R.K. Bajpai	Allahabad (N)	GEN	INC
11	R.R. Devi	Jahangiri Ganj	SC	INC
12	Raj Pati Devi	Gauri Ganj	GEN	INC
13	Rama	Almora	GEN	INC
14	S.C. Guriya	Kashimpur	GEN	INC
15	S.K. Bakshi	Lucknow (E)	GEN	INC
16	S.K. Dubey	Birapur	GEN	INC
17	Santosh K. Pathak	Dataganj	GEN	INC
18	Saraswati Devi	Bageshwar	SC	INC
19	Shakuntala	Harora	SC	INC
20	Shyama Devi	Basti	GEN	INC
21	Sukhda Mishra	Etawah	GEN	INC
22	Sunita Chauhan	Rai Bareli	GEN	INC

Total seats = 425

Source : Statistical Report On General Election,1974 to the Legislative Assembly of U.P. Election Commission of India, New Delhi. And *Who's Who* 1974 published by Vidhan Sabha.

U.P Assembly Elections-Elected Women Legislator 1969

SNo	*Candidate's Name*	*Constituency*	*Category*	*Party*
1	Asha Singh	Hardoi	GEN	INC
2	Gaytri Devi	Iglas	GEN	BKD
3	H. Habibullah	Hader Garh	GEN	INC
4	Indra Mohini	Chandausi	GEN	INC
5	K. Begurn	Sandila	GEN	INC
6	Kala Rani	Bilgram	GEN	INC
7	Manwali Devi	Bikapur	GEN	INC
8	Masali Devi	Bansgaon	GEN	SSP
9	Pyari	Pharanda	GEN	INC
10	R. Kishori	Basti	GEN	INC
11	R.K. Bajpai	Allahabad (N)	GEN	INC
12	Raj Pati Devi	Gauri Ganj	GEN	INC

S.No	*Candidate's Name*	*Constituency*	*Category*	*Party*
13	S. Kurnari	Data Ganj	SC	INC
14	Saraswati Devi	Bageswar	GEN	INC
15	Shakuntala	Harora	SC	INC
16	Sia Dulari	Manikpur	SC	INC
17	Subhagya Wati	Aonla	GEN	BKD
18	Vidyawati	Mohammada	GEN	INC

Total Seat = 425

Source : Statistical Report On General Election , 1969 to the Legislative Assembly of U.P. Election Commission of India, New Delhi. And *Who's Who* 1969 published by Vidhan Sabha.

U.P Assembly Elections-Elected Women Legislator 1967

SNo	*Candidate's Name*	*Constituency*	*Category*	*Party*
1	Beni Bai	Mauranipur	GEN	INC
2	Indra Mohini	Chandausi	GEN	INC
3	Jasoda	Dhuriapur	SC	SC
4	Kala Rani	Bilgrama	GEN	INC
5	Masali Devi	Bansgoa	GEN	SSP
6	R.K. Bajpai	Allahabad (N)	GEN	INC
7	Shakuntala	Harora	SC	INC

Total seats = 425

Source : Statistical Report On General Election,1967 to the Legislative Assembly of U.P. Election Commission of India, New Delhi. And *Who's Who* 1967 published by Vidhan Sabha.

UP Assembly Elections-Elected Women Legislator 1962

SNo	*Candidate's Name*	*Constituency*	*Category*	*Party*
1	Beni Bai	Mau	SC	INC
2	Brij Rani Devi	Bithoor	GEN	INC
3	Champawati	Fatehpur	GEN	INC
4	Genda Devi	Khalilabad	SC	INC
5	Jasoda	Dhuriapur	SC	INC
6	Kala Rani	Bilgram	GEN	INC
7	Kishwar Aro	Rampur C	GEN	INC
8	P. Kishori	Basti	GEN	INC
9	Prakash Wati Sood	Meerut Ca	GEN	INC
10	R.K. Bajpai	Allahabad	GEN	INC
11	R.R. Devi	Akbarpur	SC	INC
12	S. Nayar	Nagar	GEN	BJS

S.No	Candidate's Name	Constituency	Category	Party
13	S. Rohatgi	Kanpur Ci	GEN	INC
14	Shakuntala	Sarsawa	SC	INC
15	Shradha Devi	Kithore	GEN	INC
16	Sia Dulari	Manikpur	SC	INC
17	Sucheta Kripalani	Mandhwal	GEN	INC
18	Tara Aggarwal	Kanpur Ci	GEN	INC
19	V. Lakshmi	Deoprayag	GEN	INC
20	Vidyawati	Bah	GEN	INC

Total Seats = 430

Source: Report on the 3rd General Election in India 1962, Election Commission of India, New Delhi.

UP Assembly Elections-Elected Women Legislator 1957

SNo	Candidate's Name	Constituency	Category	Party
1	Amola Devi	Atheha	GEN	INC
2	Beni Bai	Mau	SC	INC
3	Bindumati Devi	Pratab Ganj	GEN	INC
4	Brij Rani Devi	Bilhaur	GEN	INC
5	Chandrawati	Bijnore	SC	INC
6	Dulara Devi	Fakharpur	SC	INC
7	Genda Devi	Khalillabad	SC	INC
8	K.K. Goindi	Karchana	GEN	INC
9	Jasoda	Bansogaon	SC	INC
9	Kailashwati	Chillupar	GEN	INC
10	Prabhawati Devi	Lambhua	GEN	INC
11	Prakash Wati Sood	Meerut Cantt.	GEN	INC
12	R. Kishori	Domariaganj	GEN	INC
13	R.R. Devi	Akabarpur	SC	INC
14	Sajjan Devi Manhot	Shoorpur	GEN	JAN
15	Saraswati Devi	Sarju	GEN	INC
16	Satyavati	Dadri	GEN	INC
17	Shakuntala	Harora	SC	INC
18	Shradha Devi	Kithore	GEN	INC
19	Sukhrani	Fatehpur	SC	INC
20	Sunita Chauhan	Salon	GEN	INC
21	Tara Devi	Mariahu	GEN	INC
22	V. Bajpai	Shahabad	GEN	INC
23	V. Lakshmi	Deoprayag	GEN	INC

Total Seat = 341

Source : Report on the 2nd General Election in India 1957. Page: 946-1011, Election Commission of India. New Delhi.

U.P Assembly Elections-Elected Women Legislator 1952

SNo	*Candidate's Name*	*Constituency*	*Category*	*Party*
1	Asha Lata Vyas	Phulpur (So	SC	INC
2	Brij Rani Devi	Akbarpur (13	GEN	INC
3	Chandrawati	Bijnore Cen	SC	INC
4	Jamuna	Chajipur	GEN	INC
5	Jasoda	Banagaon	SC	INC
6	Laxmi Devi	Sandila	GEN	RRP
7	Paremeshari Devi	Jaunpur(So	GEN	INC
8	Prakash Wati Sood	Hapur Nort	SC	INC
9	Sajjan Devi Manhot	Gonda (East	GEN	INC
10	Savitri Devi	Masafirkha	GEN	INC
11	Vidyawati	Eatah East	GEN	INC

Total Seat = 347

Source : Report On the General Election in India 1952, Election Commission of India, New Delhi.

APPENDIX-3

NAME OF THE WOMEN LEGISLATOR WHO WERE ELECTED MORE THAN ONCE

S.No	*Candidate's Name*	*No. of Times Elected*
1	A. Ammal	2
2	Beni Bai	6
3	Brij Rani Devi	3
4	Champawati	2
5	Chandrawati	2
6	Dulara Devi	2
7	Gauri Devi	3
8	Gaytri Devi	2
9	Genda Devi	5
10	Gulab Devi	3
11	Gyanwati Singh	2
12	Indra Mohini	3
13	Jasoda	4
14	Jyostana Srivastava	2
15	K. Begum	4
16	K. Dariyawadi	2
17	Kala Rani	3
18	Kamla Sahani	3
19	Krishna Rawat	2
20	Masali Devi	2
21	Mayavati Persad	2
22	Mayawati	4
23	Omwati Devi	3
24	P. Tiwari	2
25	Padma Seth	3
26	Parwati Devi	2
27	Prakash Wati Sood	3
28	Prem Lata Katiyar	4
29	Premwati	2
30	Pushpa Devi	3
31	R. Kishori	2
32	R.K. Bajpai	4
33	R.R. Devi	4
34	Raj Laxmi Verma	2

35	Raj Pati Devi	5
36	S. Nayar	2
37	S.K. Bakshi	4
38	Sajjan Devi Manhot	2
39	Santosh K. Pathak	3
40	Saraswati Devi	3
41	Saraswati Tiwari	2
42	Savitri Devi	3
43	Shakuntal	5
44	Sharda Devi	4
45	Shradha Devi	3
46	Sia Dulari	3
47	Sukh Devi Verma	3
48	Sukhda Mishra	4
49	Sunita Chauhan	4
50	Uma Tripathi	2
51	Urmila Devi Yadav	2
52	Urmila Rajput	2
53	V. Lakshmi	4
54	Vidyawati	3
55	Vijaya Yadav	2
56	Vimala Rakesh	4

Source: Prepared from the Statistical Reports (1952-2002) General Election to Assembly of UP and Who's Who published by UP Vidhan Sabha secreteriat (1952-2002).

Detailed List of Candidates Elected More than Once

Candidate's Name	*Year*
A. Ammal	1980
A. Ammal	1985
BeniBai	1980
Beni Bai	1985
Beni Bai	1974
Beni Bai	1967
Beni Bai	1962
Beni Bai	1957
Brij Rani Devi	1962
Brij Rani Devi	1952
Brij Rani Devi	1957
Champawati	1962
Champawati	1974
Chandrawati	1952
Chandrawati	1957
Dulara Devi	1957

Dulara Devi	1974
Gauri Devi	1980
Gauri Devi	1996
Gauri Devi	1989
Gaytri Devi	1974
Gaytri Devi	1969
Genda Devi	1962
Genda Devi	1974
Genda Devi	1980
Genda Devi	1985
Genda Devi	1957
Gulab Devi	2002
Gulab Devi	1991
Gulab Devi	1996
Gyanwatl Singh	1996
Gyanwati Singh	1991
Indra Mohini	1969
Indra Mohini	1967
Indra Mohini	1974
Jasoda 1952	
Jasoda 1957	
Jasoda 1962	
Jasoda 1967	
Jyostana Srivastava	1993
Jyostana Srivastava	1991
K. Begum	1985
K. Begum	1980
K. Begum	1977
K. Begum	1969
K. Dariyawadi	1985
K. Dariyawadi	1980
Kala Rani	1962
Kala Rani	1967
Kala Rani	1969
Kamla Sahani	1989
Kamla Sahani	1985
Kamla Sahani	1980
Krishna Rawat	1996
Krishna Rawat	1985
Masali Devi	1967
Masali Devi	1969
Mayavati Persad	1996
Mayavati Persad	2002
Mayawati	1996
Mayawati	2002
Mayawati	2002
Mayawati	1996
Omwati Devi	1985
Omwati Devi	2002

Candidate's Name	*Year*
Omwati Devi	1996
P Tiwari	1985
P. Tiwari	1980
Padma Seth	1989
Padma Seth	1991
Padma Seth	1985
Parwati Devi	1974
Parwati Devi	1980
Prakash Wati Sood	1962
Prakash Wati Sood	1957
Prakash Wati Sood	1952
Prem Lata. Katiyar	1993
Prem Lata. Katiyar	1991
Prem Lata Katiyar	1996
Prem Lata Katiyar	2002
Premwati	1989
Premwati	1980
Pushpa Devi	1989
Pushpa Devi	1977
Pushpa Devi	1985
R. Kishori	1957
R. Kishori	1969
R.K. Bajpai	1974
R.K. Bajpai	1969
R.K. Bajpai	1962
R.K. Bajpai	1967
R.R. Devi	1957
R.R. Devi	1962
R.R. Devi	1974
R.R. Devi	1977
Raj Laxmi Verma	1993
Raj Laxmi Verma	2002
Raj Pati Devi	1989
Raj Pati Devi	1985
Raj Pati Devi	1980
Raj Pati Devi	1974
Raj Pati Devi	1969
S. Nayar	1977
S. Nayar	1962
S.K. Bakshi	1985
S.K. Bakshi	1977
S.K. Bakshi	1980
S.K. Bakshi	1974
Sajjan Devi Manhot	1957
Sajjan Devi Manhot	1952
Santosh K. Pathak	1980

Candidate's Name	*Year*
Santosh K. Pathak	1974
Santosh K. Pathak	1989
Saraswati Devi	1957
Saraswati Devi	1969
Saraswati Devi	1974
Saraswati Tiwari	1989
Saraswati Tiwari	1985
Savitri Devi	1989
Savitri Devi	1952
Savitri Devi	1993
Shakuntala	1967
Shakuntala	1962
Shakuntala	1974
Shakuntala	1957
Shakuntala	1969
Sharda Devi	1985
Sharda Devi	1989
Sharda Devi	1977
Sharda Devi	1991
Shradha Devi	2002
Shradha Devi	1957
Shradha Devi	1962
Sia Dulari	1969
Sia Dulari	1989
Sia Dulari	1962
Sukh Devi Verma	2002
Sukh Devi Verma	1996
Sukh Devi Verma	1993
Sukhda Mishra	1989
Sukhda Mishra	1974
Sukhda Mishra	1980
Sukhda Mishra	1985
Sunita Chauhan	1957
Sunita Chauhan	1974
Sunita Chauhan	1980
Sunita Chauhan	1977
Uma Tripathi	1985
Uma Tripathi	1977
Urmila Devi Yadav	1996
Urmila Devi Yadav	1993
Urmila Rajput	1993
Urmila Rajput	1991
V. Lakshmi	1962
V. Lakshmi	1985
V. Lakshmi	1989
V. Lakshmi	1957

Candidate's Name	*Year*
Vidyawati	1969
Vidyawati	1962
Vidyawati	1952
Vijaya Yadav	2002
Vijaya Yadav	1996
Vimala Rakesh	1991
Vimala Rakesh	1989
Vimala Rakesh	1985
Vimala Rakesh	1980

Total number of candidates elected more than once is 56 and seen at 166 places in the list

Source: Prepared from the Stastiscal Report (1952-2002) General Election to Assembly of UP and Who's Who published by UP Vidban Sabha Secreteriat (1952-2002).

APPENDIX-4

LIST OF WOMEN LEGISLATORS WHO WERE CABINET MINISTERS, STATE MINISTERS AND DEPUTY MINISTERS IN DIFFERENT COUNCILS OF MINISTERS

First Legislative Assembly 1952

Pt. Govind Ballabh Pant Cabinet	Zero
Dr. Sampurnanand Cabinet	Zero

Second Legislative Assembly 1957

Dr. Sampurnanand Cabinet	
1. Smt. Prakashvati Sood	DY CM
Shri Chandrabhan Gupta Cabinet	
1. Smt. Sucheta Kripalani	Minister
2. Smt. Prakashvati Sood	Dy. Minister

Third Legislative Assembly 1962

Shri Chandrabhan Gupta Cabinet	
1. Smt. Sucheta Kripalani	Minister
2. Smt. Prakashvati Sood	Dy. Minister
3. Smt. Tara Agrawal	Sabha Secy.
Smt. Sucheta Kripalani Cabinet	
1. Smt Tara Agrawal	Assembly Secy.

Fourth Legislative Assembly 1967

Shri Chandra Bhanu Gupta Cabinet	Zero
Shri Charan Singh Cabinet	Zero

Fifth Legislative Assembly 1969

Shri Chandrabhanu Gupta Cabinet	
1. Smt. Vidyavati Rathaur	Minister
2. Smt. Kudsia Begum	Minister
3. Smt. Sia Dulari	Dy. Minister
4. Smt. Indra Mohini	Dy. Minister
Shri Charan Singh Cabinet	
1. Smt. Vidyavati Rathaur	Minister
2. Dr. Smt. Rajendra Kumari Vajpayee	State Minister
Shri T.N. Singh Cabinet	

1. Smt. Kudsia Begum	Minister
2. Smt. Indra Mohini	Dy. Minister
Shri Kamalapati Tripathi Cabinet	
1. Dr. Rajendra Kumari Vajpayee	Minister
2. Smt. Begum Hamida Habibulla	State Minister
Shri Hemavati Nandan Bahuguna Cabinet	
1. Dr. Rajendra Kumari Vajpayee	Minister
2. Smt. Mohsina Kidwai	State Minister

Sixth Legislative Assembly 1974

Shri Hemavati Nandan Bahuguna Cabinet	
1. Dr. Rajendra Kumari Vajpayee	Minister
2. Smt. Mohsina Kidwai	Minister
Shri Narayan Dutta Tiwari Cabinet	
1. Dr. Rajendra Kumari Vajpayee	Minister
2. Smt. Mohsina Kidwai	Minister
3. Smt. Indra Mohini	State Minister

Seventh Legislative Assembly 1977

Shri Ramnaresh Yadav Cabinet	
1. Smt. Chandravati	Minister
2. Smt. Shakuntala Nair	State Minister
3. Smt. Malati Sharma	Dy. Minister
Shri Banarasi Das Cabinet	
1. Smt. Chandravati	Minister

Eighth LegislativeAssembly 1980

Shri Vishwanath Pratap Singh Cabinet	
1. Smt. Swaroop Kumari Bakhshi	State Minister
2. Smt. Premvati Tiwari	State Minister
Shri Sripati Mishra Cabinet	
1. Smt. Swaroop Kumari Bakhshi	State Minister
2. Smt. Indra Mohini	State Minister
3. Smt. Sunita Chauhan	State Minister
4. Smt. Premvati Tiwari	State Minister
5. Smt. Beni Bai	State Minister
Shri Narayan Dutta Tiwari Cabinet	
1. Smt. Sunita Chauhan	State Minister
2. Smt. Premvati Tiwari	State Minister
3. Smt. Beni Bai	State Minister
4. Km. Saraswati Ammal	Dy. Minister

Ninth Legislative Assembly 1989

Shri Narayan Dutta Tiwari Cabinet	
1. Smt. Swaroop Kumari Bakhshi	Minister
2. Smt. Beni Bai	Minister
3. Smt. Padma Seth	State Minister
4. Smt. Sukhada Mishra	Minister
Shri Vir Bahadur Singh Cabinet	
1. Smt. Swaroop Kumari Bakhshi	Minister

2. Smt. Sushila Rohtagi	Minister
3. Smt. Padma Seth	State Minister
4. Ku. Sarasvati Ammal	State Minister
5. Smt. Deepa Kaul	State Minister
6. Smt. Pramila Baddhwar Mehra	Dy. Minister
Shri Narayan Datta Tiwari Cabinet	
1. Smt. Swaroop Kumari Bakhshi	Minister
2. Smt. Sushila Rohtagi	Minister
3. Smt. Beni Bai	Minister
4. Smt Hitesh Kumari	Dy. Minister
5. Smt. Deepa Kaul	State Minister
6. Smt. Pramila Baddhwar Mehra	Dy. Minister
7. Smt. Reena Kumari	Dy. Minister
10th Legislative Assembly 1989	
Shri Mulayam Singh Cabinet	
1. Smt. Sukhada Mishra	Minister
11th Legislative Assembly 1991	
Shri Kalyan Singh Cabinet	
1. Smt. Premavatilata Katiyar	Minister
2. Smt. Sharada Chauhan	State Minister
12th Legislative Assembly 1993	
Shri Mulayam Singh Cabinet	
Miss Mayavati, Cabinet	
1. Smt. Sushila	Minister
13th Legislative Assembly 1996	
Miss Mayavati Cabinet	
1. Smt. Prabha Diwedi	Minister
2. Smt. Raj Rai Singh	State Minister
Shri Kalyan Singh Cabinet	
1. Smt. Prabha Diwedi	Minister
2. Smt. Premalata Katiyar	Minister
3. Smt. Gulab Devi	State Minister
4. Smt. Raj Rai Singh	State Minister
14th Legislative Assembly 2002	
Miss Mayavati Cabinet	
1. Anuradha Chaudhry	Minister
2. Seema Rizvee	State Minister

APPENDIX-5

AFTER IMPLEMENTATION OF THE CONSTITUTION OF INDIA, FROM 5TH MAY 1952 TO 7TH JULY 1982, THE FOLLOWING WOMEN WERE ELECTED TO THE LEGISLATIVE COUNCIL OF U.P.

1. Smt. Inderamohini
2. Smt. Indira Haridyesh
3. Smt. Kamala Tyagi
4. Smt Kudesia Begum
5. Smt. Chandrawati
6. Smt. Tara Agrawal
7. Smt. Dayawati
8. Kum. Daya Bahan
9. Smt Deepa Kaul
10. Smt. Premwati Tiwari
11. Smt Prabhawati
12. Smt. Prabhashim
13. Smt. Begum Mohisina Khalal Kidwai
14. Smt. Mahadevi Verma
15. Smt. Maya Chaudhary
16. Smt. Malati Pandey
17. Smt. Rani Lila Ranikumar Bhargaw
18. Smt. Vidya Vajpayee
19. Smt. Vidyawati Rathor
20. Smt. Veena Duggal
21. Smt. Shakuntala Srivastava
22. Smt. Shakuntala Devi
23. Smt. Shantabai Kher
24. Smt. Shanti Devi w/o Late Shri Sharda Prasad
25. Smt. Shanti Devi w/o Chaudhari Badan Singh
26. Smt. Shanti Devi Agrawal
27. Smt. Shivrajwati Nehru
28. Smt. Sheela Kaul
29. Km. Satya Sood
30. Km. Saraswati Ammal
31. Smt. Savitri Shyam
32. Smt. Sia Dulari

33. Smt. Sucheta Kripalani
34. Smt. Sunita Chauhan
35. Smt. Syed Jahan Begum Makaphi
36. Smt. Santosh Kumari Kapoor

Out of 457 members, women were only 36 during this period.

Thus, their representation was only 7.8 per cent in the Legislative Council. According to 1992 position, the latest list of women members Legislative Council is as under :

1. Smt. Indira Hridyesh
2. Smt. Kamla Tyagi
3. Smt. Deepa
4. Smt. Maharani Dohare
5. Smt. Vidya Vajpayee
6. Smt. Shakuntala Devi
7. Smt. Sushila Rohatagi

List of women who were elected as members of the Council in pre-independence era:

Sl.	*Name of the Legislators*	*Period*
1.	Begum Ajaj Rasool known as Smt. Kudesia Begum	1937-1952
2.	Smt. Phool Kumari Rani Sahiba	1940-52
3.	Smt. Meena Chandrawati Gupta	1937-45
4.	Smt. Shanti Devi	1950-55
5.	Smt. Sakeenatul Fatima known as Lady Vazeer Hasan	1937-49

According to the Government of India Act, 1935 the 228 members in Legislative Council of UP were to be elected from 16 kinds of areas/regions/ constituencies. There were six seats reserved for women, out of these six, one for general urban woman, three for general rural women and one each for Muslim urban woman and Muslim rural woman. In 1937, 12 women members (5.26%) were elected to the Council :

1. Smt. Uma Nehru, Farukhabad
2. Smt. Jagdamba Devi Maharani, Faizabad
3. Smt. Parvati Kumari Rajmata
4. Smt. Prakashwati Sood
5. Smt. Dr. Bolar Thungama
6. Smt. Laxmi Devi
7. Smt. Vijay Laxmi
8. Smt. Vidyawati Rathaur
9. Smt. Sharmda Tyagi
10. Begum Shahid Husain
11. Smt. Shuniti Devi
12. Smt. Satyawati Devi

Similarly, only nine (3.94%) women members were elected in the year 1942. The list of their names is as under:

1. Smt. Poornima Banerjee
2. Smt. Prakaswati Sood
3. Begum Abdulla Wazid
4. Begum Mohmed Ali
5. Smt. Laxmi Devi
6. Smt. Vijay Laxmi Pandit
7. Smt. Vidyawati Rathaur
8. Smt. Sajjan Devi Mehnot
9. Smt. Sucheta Kripalani

SOCIO-ECONOMIC BACKGROUND OF LEGISLATORS

Profile of the Women Legislators

S.No.	*Occupation*	*No. of Women Legislators*	*Percentage*
1	Agriculture	55	57.90
2	Teacher	9	09.45
3	Lawyer	4	04.21
4	Business	5	05.26
5	House wife	11	11.53
6	Political/ Social workers	11	11.53
7	Others	7	07.32
8	Total	95	100.00

Distribution of Women Legislators based On Children

S. No.	*No. of Children*	*Number of Women*	*% age*
1	1	7	07.37
2	2	19	20.00
3	3	17	17.90
4	4	22	23.15
5	5-6	20	21.05
6	7-8	3	03.16
7	10	1	01.05
8	Unmarried	6	06.32
	Total	95	100.00

Educational Background of Women Legislators in UP Assembly

S. No.	*Educational Level*	*Number of Legislators*	*%age*
1	Under Matriculate	13	13.68
2	Matriculate	16	16.84
3	Higher Secondary/	16	16.85

	Intermediate		
4	Graduate	11	11.57
5	Graduates with LL.B.	9	09.47
6	Graduates with B.Ed.	8	08.43
7	Post-Graduate	15	15.79
8	Postgraduates with Technical qualifications	5	05.27
9	Doctors degree holders	2	02.10
	Total	95	100.00

Distribution of Women Legislators by Age Group

S. No.	*Age at Marriage*	*Number of Women*	*%age*	*Age at Entering Assembly*	*Number of Women*	*%age*
1	8-11	4	4.22	25-30	15	17.91
2	12-14	9	9.47	31-35	14	14.74
3	15-18	38	40.00	36-40	27	28.42
4	19-21	17	17.92	41-45	15	15.79
5	22-24	6	6.31	46-50	5	5.26
6	25-27	6	6.31	51-55	6	6.32
7	28-31	0	0.00	56-60	3	3.15
8	32-33	2	2.10	61-65	2	2.10
9	Unmarried	6	6.31	66-70	1	1.05
10	Other	7	7.36	71-75	5	5.26
	Total	95	100.00	Total	95	100.0

Socio-Economic Backgrounds of Respondents

S. No.	*Name*	*Age at Marriage*	*Age at entering politics*	*Education*	*Caste*	*Occupation*	*Children*
1	Omwati	16	36	literate	SC	Agriculture	–
2	Gulab Devi	33	36	MA	SC	Teaching	2F
3	Suman Lata	16	40	MA	GEN	Medical	1F+1M
4	Raj Rai Singh	20	38	BA	GEN	Self Employee	1F+3M
5	Krishna Raj	17	28	BA	SC	Agriculture	1F+1M
6	Maya Prasad	18	35	Inter	SC	Agriculture	1F+2M
7	Manju Singh	13	34	Inter	GEN	Agriculture / business	1 F+3M
8	Seema Dewedi	21	26	BA	GEN	Agriculture	1M
9	PL Katiyar	14	45	BA	OBC	Agriculture	3F+1M
10	Sukh Devi Verma	10	36	High school	SC	Agriculture	1F+4M
11	Urmila Devi	14	38	BA	OBC	Agriculture	1F+2M

12	Mithilesh Kri	21	27	Inter	SC	Agriculture	3M
13	Ramsakhi	8	38	High SChool	SC	House wife	2F+2M
14	Shusila Devi	16	57	Inter	GEN	Agriculture	2F+2M
15	Mayawati	unmarr-ied	30	BA B Ed LLB	SC	Politics	–
16	Prabha Dewedi	26	61	BA BT	GEN	Retired from govt. service	1F+2M
17	Sushila Saroj	12	39	BA B.Ed LLB	SC	Business	3F
18	Raj L. Verma	21	42	BA	OBC	Business	1F+1M
19	Prabha Rawat	15	38	Literate	OBC	Agriculture	3F+1M
20	Jyotsana Srivastava	33	54	MA Ph.D	GEN	Agriculture	1F+1M
21	Savitri Devi	12	40	H.SChool	OBC	Agriculture	4F+2M
22	Rekha Chhanghra	17	30	H School	SC	Politics	3F+1M
23	Urmila Rajput	16	37	BA LLB	GEN	Lawyer	1F+2M
24	Shashi Bala Pundir	22	36	BSCLLB	GEN	Agriculture	1M
25	Shashi Bala Bharti	26	43	MA BEd	SC	Journalism	2F+2M
26	Padama Seth	23	63	BA	GEN	Social work	4F
27	Neelam Singh	15	38	Inter	GEN	Agriculture	2F+4M
28	Sharda Devi	19	25	Literate	SC	Agriculture	2F+1M
29	Vimala Rakesh	15	35	H School	SC	Agriculture	1F
30	Kamala Sahani	18	38	MA BEd	OBC	Agriculture	2F
31	Chander Kali Verma	15	38	literate	OBC	Agriculture	5M
32	Pushpa Devi	25	36	literate	OBC	Agriculture	1F+1M
33	Premwati	28	53	MA	OBC	Public Service	1M
34	Rajpati Devi	15	36	Jr. H. School	GEN	Agriculture	3F+3m
35	Rameshewari	15	36	H. School	SC	House wife	2F+3M
36	Laljhari Devi	18	41	H.School	GEN	Agriculture	6F+2M
37	V. Lakshmi	12	37	H.Schoot	GEN	Agriculture	2F+1M
38	Shashi Mittal	19	40	BA	GEN	Agriculture	3F+1M

39	Santosh K. Pathak	13	25	Inter	GEN	Agriculture	2F+2M
40	Saraswati Tiwari	17	55	Inter	GEN	Social work	3F+1M
41	Sia Dulari	11	26	MA	SC	Agriculture	SF+3M
42	Kalarani Mishra	16	39	BALT	GEN	Social worker	2F+4M
43	K Begum	21	28	BA	OBC	Politics	2F+2M
44	Krishna Rawat	-	42	BA LLB	SC	Lawyer	
45	SK Bakshi	21	55	MA	GEN	Teaching	1F
46	Sukhda Mishra	16	33	B Sc	GEN	Agriculture	1F+1M
47	Genda Devi	18	23	H School	SC	Agriculture	4M
48	Shash Sharma	24	33	BSc MEd LLB	GEN	Agriculture	2F
49	Ashraf Immam	19	54	BA	OBC	Agriculture	5M
50	K Daryabadi	17	47	Literate	SC	Politics	3F+7M
51	Beni Bai	20	27	BA	SC	Agriculture	1F+1M
52	U Agnihotri	-	40	BA LLB	GEN	Lawyer	–
53	Hitesh Kumari	18	43	MA	OBC	Agriculture	3F+3M
54	Vimala Singh	16	43	BA	GEN	Agriculture	2M
55	Saroj Verma	18	48	BA	GEN	Agriculture	1F+2M
56	Charu Shila	16	69	Inter	GEN	Business	3F+3M
57	Reena Kumari	19	25	BA	GEN	Agriculture	1F+1M
58	Permila Bhadwar	18	42	BA	GEN	business	2F
59	Kanti Singh Vesien	20	43	H School	GEN	Agriculture	3F+2M
60	Uma Tripathi	20	46	MA	GEN	Politics	1F+2M
61	Ram Nandini Verma	17	31	H. School	GEN	Agriculture	2F+2M
62	Kamala Devi	15	53	Literate	GEN	Agriculture	2F+1M
63	Sunita Chauhan	15	27	BA	GEN	Agriculture	2F+2M
64	Kishori Shukla	11	36	Inter	GEN	Agriculture	2F+3M
65	Ghanesewari Devi	15	60	Inter	GEN	Agriculture	1F+5M
66	Suman Lata Dikshit	-	25	MA M.Ed	GEN	Politics	–

67	Pushpa Chauhan	27	42	MA	GEN	Agricultu	1F+1M
68	Yashoda Devi	13	37	Literate	GEN	Agriculture	3F+1M
69	Maharani Dohre	23	31	MA BEd	SC	Agriculture	3F+lM
70	Shashi Prabha	15	45	Inter	GEN	Agriculture	1F+2M
71	Shakuntala Naiyer	22	38	Inter	GEN	Politics	1M
72	Pushpa Talwar	17	48	MA LLB		Teaching	1F+1M
73	Malti Sharma	17	47	MA	GEN	Politics	–
74	Rama Pant Kumari	-	40	MA	GEN	Politics	–
75	Indra Mohini	19	36	BA	GEN	Politics	1F+1M
76	Kailash Pati	12	31	Inter	SC	Teaching	–
77	S K Dubey	15	43	Inter	GEN	Agriculture	2F+4M
78	Mohishina Kidwai	21	42	Inter	OBC	Politics	3F
79	Dulara Devi	15	23	–	SC	Agriculture	2F+2M
80	Shyama Devi	16	32		GEN	Agriculture	3F+2M
81	R K Bajpai	22	35	MAPHD	GEN	Politics	1F+1M
82	Champawati	15	35	H School	GEN	Agriculture	3F+2M
83	Gayatri Devi	15	40	BA	GEN	Agriculture	5F+1M
84	Ganga Devi	15	40	Inter	SC	Agriculture	3F+5M
85	Manwati Devi	17	44	H School	GEN	Agriculture	2F+4M
86	Vidyawati Rathore	17	35	H School-	GEN	Politics	–
87	Shakuntala Devi	15	35	BA	SC	Teaching	–
88	Parkashwati Sood	18	35	H School	GEN	Politics	1M
89	Brijrani Mishra	15	34	H Schol	GEN	Politics	2F+1M
90	Tara Aggarwal	15	39	Inter	GEN	Politics	1F+2M
91	S Rohatgi	26	41	MA	GEN	Teaching	3F+2M
92	Sucheta Kripalani	26	40	MA	GEN	Teaching	–
93	Chandervati	20	20	BA LLB	GEN	Politics	1F+1M
94	K K Goindi	-	35	MA LT	GEN	Teaching	–
95	Sajjan Devi Manhot	13	25	Literate	GEN	Politics	IF+3M

APPENDIX- 7

EDUCATIONAL AND FAMILY BACKGROUND AND EMERGENCE OF WOMEN AS LEADERS

S. No.	*Name*	*Marital status*	*Widow*	*Education*	*Caste*	*Religion*	*Emergence as leader*
1	Omwati	Married		–	SC	Hindu	Social worker
2	Gulab Devi	Married		MA	SC	Hindu	Political activist
3	Suman Lata	Married		MA	GEN	Hindu	Social worker
4	Raj Rai Singh	Married		BA	GEN	Hindu	Family linkage
5	Krishna Raj	Married		BA	SC	Hindu	Social worker
6	Maya Prasad	Married		Inter-	SC	Hindu	Social worker
7	Manju Singh		Widow	Inter	GEN	Hindu	Widow Succession
8	Seema Dewedi	Married		BA	GEN	Hindu	Social worker
9	PL Katiyar		Widow	BA	OBC	Hindu	Widow Succession
10	Sukh Devi Verma		Widow	High school	SC	Hindu	Widow Succession
11	Urmila Devi		Widow	BA	OBC	Hindu	Widow Succession
12	Mithilesh Kri	Married		Inter	SC	Hindu	Social worker
13	Ramsakhi	Married		High School	SC	Hindu	Social worker
14	Shusila Devi	Married		Inter	GEN	Hindu	Social worker
15	Maya wati	Unmarried		BA B Ed LLB	SC	–	Political activist
16	Prabha Dewedi		Widow	BA BT	GEN	Hindu	Widow Succession
17	Sushila Saroj	Married		BA B.Ed LLB	SC	Hindu	Family linkage
18	Raj L.Venna	Married		BA	OBC	Hindu	Social worker
19	Prabha Rawat		Widow		OBC	Hindu	Widow Succession
20	Jyotsana Srivastava	Married		MA PhD	GEN	Hindu	Family linkage
21	Savitri Devi	Married		H.School	OBC	Hindu	Family linkage

S. No.	Name	Marital status	Widow	Education	Caste	Religion	Emergence as leader
22	Rekha Chhanghra	Married		H School	SC	Hindu	Political activist
23	Urmila Rajput	Married		BA LLB	GEN	Hindu	Political activist
24	Shashi Bala Pundir	Married		BSc LLB	GEN	Hindu	Student activist
25	Shashi Bala	Married		MA BEd	SC	Hindu	Political activist
26	Padama Seth	Married		BA	GEN	Hindu	Political activist
27	Neelam singh		Widow	Inter	GEN	Hindu	Widow. Succession
28	Sharda Devi	Married		Literate	SC	Hindu	Political activist
29	Vimala Rakesh		Widow	H School	SC	Hindu	Family linkage
30	Kamala Sahani		Widow	MA BEd	OBC	Hindu	Widow Succession
31	Chander Kali Verma		Widow	Literate	OBC	Hindu	Widow Succession
32	Pushpa Devi		Widow	Literate	OBC	Hindu	Widow Succession
33	Prem wati		Widow	Literate	OBC	Hindu	Widow Succession
34	Rajpati Devi	Married		Jr. H School	GEN	Hindu	Family linkage
35	Rameshwari	Married		H School	SC	Hindu	Social worker
36	Laljhari Devi		Widow	H School	GEN	Hindu	Widow Succession
37	V. Lakshmi		Widow	H School	GEN	Hindu	Widow Succession
38	Shashi Mittal		Widow	BA	GEN	Hindu	Widow Succession
39	Santosh K. Pathak	Married		Inter	GEN	Hindu	Political activist
40	Saraswati Tiwari	Married		Inter	GEN	Hindu	Family linkage
41	Sia Dulari	Married		BA	SC	Hindu	Political activist
42	P. Singhal	Married				Hindu	
43	K. Begum	Married		BA	OBC	Hindu	Political activist
44	Krishna Rawat	Unmarried		BA LLB	SC	Hindu	Social worker
45	SK Bakshi		Widow	MA	GEN	Hindu	Family linkage
46	Sukhda Mishra	Married		B Sc	GEN	Hindu	Family linkage
47	Genda Devi	Married		H School	SC	Hindu	Political activist

S. No.	Name	Marital status	Widow	Education	Caste	Religion	Emergence as leader
48	Shashi Sharma	Married		BSc MEd	GEN	Hindu LLB	Political activist
49	Ashraf Immam	Married		BA	OBC	Islam	Political activist
50	K Daryabadi		Widow	Literate	SC	Hindu	Family linkage
51	Beni Bai	Married		BA	SC	Hindu	Political activist
52	U Agnihotri	Unmarried		BA LLB	GEN	Hindu	Political activist
53	Hitesh Kumari	Married		MA	OBC	Hindu	Political activist
54	Vimala Singh	Married		BA	GEN	Hindu	Political activist
55	Saroj Verma	Married		BA	GEN	Hindu	Political activist
56	Charu Shila	Married		Inter	GEN	Hindu	Political activist
57	Reena Kumari	Married		BA	GEN	Hindu	Family linkage
58	Permila Bhadwar	Married		BA	GEN	Hindu	Family linkage
59	Kanti Singh Vesien	Married		H School	GEN	Hindu	Political activist
60	Uma Tripathi	Married		MA	GEN	Hindu	Political activist
61	Ramnandini Verma		Widow	H School	GEN	Hindu	Widow Succession
62	Kamala Devi	Married			GEN	Hindu	Widow Succession
63	Sunita Chuhan	Married		BA	GEN	Hindu	Political activist
64	Kishori Shukla	Married		Inter	GEN	Hindu	Political activist
65	Ghanesewari Devi	Married		Inter	GEN	Hindu	Family linkage
66	Suman Lata Dikshit	Unmarried		MA M.Ed	GEN	Hindu	Student activist
67	Pushpa Chauhan	Married		MA	GEN	Hindu	Family linkage
68	Premwati Tiwari	Married	Widow	MA	GEN	Hindu	Widow Succession
69	Maharani Dohre	Married		MA BEd	SC	Hindu	Political activist
70	Shashi Prabha	Married		Inter	GEN	Hindu	Family linkage
71	Shakuntala Naiyer	Married		Inter	GEN	Hindu	Family linkage
72	Pushpa Talwar	Married		MA LLB		Hindu	Political activist

S. No.	Name	Marital status	Widow	Education	Caste	Religion	Emergence as leader
73	Malti Sharma	Married		MA	GEN	Hindu	Political
74	Rama Pant Kumari	Unmarried		MA	GEN	Hindu	Political activist
75	Indra Mohini		Widow	BA	GEN	Hindu	Political activist
76	Kailash Pati		Widow	Inter	SC	Hindu	Widow Succession
77	S K Dubey	Married		Inter	GEN	Hindu	Family linkage
78	Mohishina Kidwai	Married		–	OBC	Islam	Family linkage
79	Dulara Devi		Widow		SC	Hindu	Widow Succession
80	Shyama Devi		Widow		GEN	Hindu	Widow Succession
81	R K Bajpai	Married		MA PhD		Hindu	Student activist
82	Champawati	Married		H School	GEN	Hindu	Political activist
83	Gayatri Devi		Widow	BA	GEN	Hindu	Family linkage
84	Ganga Devi	Married		Inter	SC	Hindu	Political activist
85	Manwati Devi	Married		H School	GEN	Hindu	Family linkage
86	Vidyawati Rathore	Married		H School	GEN	Hindu	Political activist
87	Shakuntala Devi	Married		BA	SC	Hindu	Political activist
88	Parkash Wati Sood	Married		H School	GEN	Hindu	Political activist
89	Brijrani Mishra	Married		H. School	GEN	Hindu	Political activist
90	Tara Aggarwal		Widow	Inter	GEN	Hindu	Political activist
91	S Rohatgi	Married		MA	GEN	Hindu	Political activist
92	Sucheta Kripalani	Married		MA	GEN	Hindu	Political activist and family links
93	Chandervati	Married		BA LLB	GEN	Hindu	Political activist
94	K K Goindi	Unmarried		MA LT	GEN	Hindu	Political activist
95	Sajjan Devi Manhot		Widow		GEN	Hindu	Political activist

APPENDIX- 8

QUESTIONNAIRE

I. Personal Information

1.1 Name
1.2 Age
1.3 Place of Birth: Urban (1), Semi-Urban (2), Rural (3), Semi-Rural (4), Remote village (5)
1.4 Educational Qualification:Uneducated (1), Pre-High School (2), High School (3), Graduate (4), Post-Graduate (5), Professional (6)
1.5 Occupation / Profession
1.6 Age at marriage: below 15 (1), 15-20 (2), 20-25 (3), 30 and above (4)
1.7 Average annual income

II. Information on Involvement in Politics

2.1 At what age did you enter politics? Why? and How?
2.2 Was there any opposition / resistance from your family at your entering politics? If yes, reason for opposition.
2.3 Are you associated with any social / public organisation? If yes, please specify the type of association.

III. Information on Association with Political Party/Parties

3.1 Why did you join this particular party? Are you its founder member?
3.2 Are you an office bearer of the party? If yes, what position do you hold?

IV. Involvement in Party and Election Politics

Election Party contested	*Constituency Name proposed by*	*Year*

* Please specify the level of election: local bodies, state legislature, national legislature.

4.1 Specify your contribution to party's women's wing.
4.2 What is your involvement in the campaign (for instance, have you been on an election campaign tour etc.) especially with women candidates?
4.3 Did you face any financial constraints to context elections? If yes, how did you manage?
4.4 What problems / constraints do you face as a 'women' in your party?
4.5 Do you have to work harder to prove your worth?
4.6 Were you ever denied a ticket because the leadership thought it ought to go to a 'male' member?
4.7 Were you ever threatened or attacked during your election campaign or otherwise during your political career? Please give instance(s).
4.8 What is the response of your male colleagues to issues raised by you?
4.9 Would you or have you taken a stand different from that of your party on certain controversial issues (e.g. Muslim Personal Law)? Please specify.

V. Role & Involvement in UP Legislative Politics & Proceedings

5.1 Why did you choose your present constituency for the recent general elections?

5.2 How many times have you visited your constituency after being elected in this general elections?
5.3 What all are you doing for the women of your constituency?
5.4 How often do you raise issues on the floor of the House?
5.5 Have you moved any resolutions / motions in the Assembly? If yes, how many times and were they passed?
5.6 Are you given a chance to speak on issues specific to women only or other issues as well?
5.7 What is the position of women as a 'group' in LT Assembly? Is there any solitary among women legislators on women's issues?
5.8 Do you think women legislators can do more for women and women specific problems than their male counterparts?
5.9 Would you want to have any 'specific' privileges for women in Assembly proceedings? If yes, please specify.
5.10 Were you ever manhandled or attacked in the Assembly?
5.11 Are you a member of any legislative committee? If yes, what is your role on this committee?

VI. Role as a Minister

6.1 Were you assigned your present portfolio or you chose it?
6.2 Do you feel you could have done better were you given a different portfolio?
6.3 Do you have adequate powers to operate and is there are room for initiative?
6.4 Have you brought any changes in your present ministry in terms of policy decisions, etc.?
6.5 How do you view your job as a minister? What problems do you face being a 'woman' minister?

VII. List out some important issues which are faced by our country in general and women in particular

7.1

Issues Involvement	*Opinion*

7.2 What do you think about the status of women in India today?
7.3 Should women be treated as a 'minority' albeit a 'large' one in the same sense as other 'minorities' in the country? Do you support the policy of 'reservation' for women?
7.4 What are your suggestions for an increased and qualitatively better participation of women in decision-making and political process?
7.5 You owe your success in politics to------------------.

BIBLIOGRAPHY

Atal, Yogesh; 1993: *Women in Politics,* Thailand, UNESCO, Principal Regional Office for Asia Pacific.

Altekar, A.S. and Puri, B; 1955: *State and Government in Ancient India,* Banaras, Motilal Banarsidas.

Altekar, A. S. 1956: *The Position of Women in Hindu Civilization,* Delhi, Patna, Varanasi, Motilal Banarsidas.

Alexander, K. C. 1968: *Social Mobility Among Pulava Harijans in Kerala,* Poona, Deccan College.

Akhter, M.J. 1999: *Iron Lady: Mayawati,* New Delhi, Bahujan Sanghatak, Gurudwara Rakabganj Road.

Aggarwal, J.C. and Chowdhry, N.K. 1996: *Election In India* 1952-96, Delhi, Shipra Publishers.

Annual Plan - Uttar Pradesh 2000-2001: Lucknow, Planning Department, Government of UP, UP Secretariat.

Baden Powell, B.H. 1896: *Indian Village Communities,* London, Longmans Green & Company.

Beteille, Andre 1992: *Society and Politics in India*, Oxford University Press Bhatt.

Bottomore,T.B. 1964: *Elite and Society,* London, Penguin Books.

Dhillon, H. S. 1955: *Leadership and Groups in South Indian Village,* New Delhi, PEO Publication, Planning Commission.

Baig, Tara Ali;1976: *Women Power,* New Delhi, S. Chand and Company (Pvt.) Ltd.

Baig, T. A. 1958: Enakshi Bhavanan (Ed), *Women of India,* New Delhi, Creative and Fine Arts, Publication Div. Government of India, pp. 169.

Bharatiya Vidhya Bhavan, 1974: "History and culture of Indian People" in *The Mughal Empire,*Vol. VII, pp. 566.

Baral, J.K. 1990: *Gender Politics: A study of socio-economic*

Conditions and political participation of working women in Orissa, New Delhi, South Asia publication.

Dahl, R.; 196 1: *Who Governs,* UK, New Heaven Press.

Dubey, S.C.; 1961: "Dominant Caste and Village Leadership", *India, Mussoorie, Paper read in Seminar on Trend of Change in Village in* ICSSR.

Down, A.; 1957: *Economic Theory of Democracy,* New York, Harper& Brothers.

Elizabeth Holtzmen and Shirley Williams; 1987: *Women in Political World: Observations, Fall, Daedalus,* pp. 28

Fishbein, Martin; 1963: "Perceptions of Non-members: A Test of Merton's Reference Group Theory", *Sociometry,* Vol.26, No.3, pp. 271-83.

Gopalan, Sarala; 1997: *Women In India: A Statistical Profile,* New Delhi, Ministry of Human Resource Development, Government of India Publication.

Gould, A. H. and Ganguly, S.; 1993: *India Votes,* Oxford, Westview Press.

Harper, E.; 1959: *Community Organization in Action,* New York, Association Press.

Hazel, D'Lama; 1983: *Women in Local Government: A Study of Maharashtra,* New Delhi, Concept Publishing Co.

Jain, Deviki; 1975: (ed) *Indian Women,* New Delhi, January, p.51.

Jain Shobha; 1984: "Women and People's Ecological Movement: A Case Study of Women's Role In Chipko Movement in Uttar Pradesh", *Economic and Political Weekly* (13 October 1984), pp: 1790.

Jharta, B.; 1996: *Women and Politics in India: Impact of family and Education on Women Political Activists*, South Asia Book, New Delhi.

Kumari Ranjana; and Dubey Anju; 1994: *Women Parliamentarians,* New Delhi, Har-Anand Publications.

Kumari, Ranjana. 1996: "Introduction", in Friedrich Ebert Stiftung (ed), *Women in Politics—Forms and Processes,* New Delhi, Har- Anand Publications, pp. 1-13.

Kumari, Ranjana; 1992: *Women in Decision Making,* Delhi, Vikas Publication.

Kaushik, Susheela; 1996: "Women and Political Participation" in Friedrich Ebert Stiftung (ed), *Women in Politics-Forms and Processes,* New Delhi, Har- Anand Publications, pp.35-53.

Kaushik, Susheela; 1993:"Women In politics in India" in Atal Yogesh (ed), *Women in Politics,* UNESCO, Regional office for Asia Pacific, Thailand, pp. 53-81.

Kaushik, Susheela; 1993: *Empowering Women,* Delhi, FES/Har Anand Publication.

Kristin, Helmore; 1985: *The Neglected Resource: Women in the Reprints,Developing World,* Boston, The Christian Science Monitor p.1.

Kamble, N.D.; 1982: *The Scheduled Castes: Their Participation in Politics,* New Delhi, Sterling Publication.

Leslie J, Calman; 1989: "Women and Movement Politics in India" *Asian Survey* (October 1989), p. 943.

Lasswell, H.D.; 1950: *Study of Power,* U.K., Glencoe Free Press.

Lasswell, H.D.; 1950: *Power & Society—A Framework for Political Enquiry,* London, Routledge and Kegan Paul.

Lewis, Oscar; 1954: *Group Dynamics in a North Indian Village,* New Delhi, Planning Commission (PEO).

Maine, H.S.; 1871: *Village Communities in the East and West,* London, John Murray.

Muni, S.D.; 1970: "Women in the Electoral Process : A Statistical Analysis of Lok Sabha" in Mazumdar Vina (ed.), *Symbol of Power: Studies on the Political Status of Women in India,* Bombay, Allied Publishers.

Mannhein, K.;1956: *Essay on the Sociology of Culture,* London, Routledge Press.

Merton, R.K.; 1968: *Social Theory and Social Structure,* New Delhi, Amerind.

Majumdar, R.C.; 1967: *An Advanced History of India,* London, New York, Macmillan and St. Martins Press.

Mohanty, K.T.; 2000: *Ewpowering Women—A Catalyst in Indian Development,* Employment News (September 16-22, 2000), New Delhi, National Weekly.

Menon, N.; 1999: *Gender and Politics in India,* Oxford University Press, Oxford.

Ministry of Education and Social Welfare; 1975: *Towards Equality: Report of the Committee on Status of Women in India.* New Delhi, p. 7.

Pravin, N. Seth;1979 : *Political Participation of Women* (1951-1979), Department of Political Science, Ph.D. Thesis, Gujarat University, Ahemdabad.

Patel, V.;1996: "Women's Participation in Policy and Decision Making Process: Need for a Network" in Friedrich Ebert Stiftung (ed), *Women in Politics—Forms and Processes,* New Delhi, Har- Anand Publications, pp. 15-35

Pant, A.D. and Kumar, B.; 1986: *Elites Perception of Socio-economic Change in Uttar Pradesh,* Allahabad, G.B. Pant Social Science Institute.

Parvathamma, C. and Jongem, T.; 1969: Indian Scheduled Caste MPs: A Socioeconomic Profile, *Journal of Karnataka University,* Vol. V (April), pp. 1-14.

Phadnis, Urmila, Malani and Indira. 1978: *Women of the World (Illusion and Reality),* New Delhi, Vikas Publishing House Pvt. Ltd.

Purushothaman, S.;1998: *The Empowerment of Women in India: Grassroots Women's Networks and the State*, New Delhi, Sage Publication.

Pandey, Sumana;1990: *Women in Politics,* Jaipur, Rawat Publications.

Raj Bala; 1997: *Scheduled Caste Leaders in Rohtak (Haryana) Sociological Inquiry,* Ph. D. Thesis, Meerut, CCS University.

Rana M.S.; 2000: *India Votes,* New Delhi, B.R. Publishing Corporation.

Srinivasan, M. A.; 1975: "Panchkanya: An Age Old Benediction", in Deviki Jain (ed.), *Indian Women,* New Delhi.

Saberwal, S.; 1971: "Social Mobility and Change in Scheduled Caste in Punjab", in Satish Saberwal (ed.), *Beyond the Village,* Simala, I.L.A.S.

Sangwan, K.S.; 1986: *"Harijan Legislatures: Awareness and Role Performance",* M.Phil Dissertation, Punjab University Chandigarh.

Singh, Y.; 1955: *The Changing Pattern of Socio-economic Relation in the Country Side,* Lucknow, Doctoral Thesis, Lucknow University.

Srinivas, M.N.; 1959: *Caste : A Trend Report and Bibliography,* Oxford, Oxford University Press.

Sarotri, G.; 1979: *Parties and Party Systems: A framework for Analysis,* Cambridge, Cambridge University Press.

Sachchidananda; 1977: The *Harijan Elites: A Study of their Status, Network and Mobility,* Faridabad, Thompson Press.

Sirsikar, V. M.; 1970: *Rural Elites in Developing Societies,* New Delhi, Orient Company Ltd.

Sanderson, D.; 1939: *Rural Community Organization,* New York, Wiley Publication

Stiftung, Friedrich Ebert; 1996: *Women in Politics—Forms and Processes,* New Delhi, HarAnand Publication.

Sara Longwe; 1996: *Gender Training Module: Unit-3,* UNICEF.

Vidyarthi, L.P.; 1967: *Leadership in India,* New Delhi, Asia Publishing House.

Young India; 1964: *The Role of Women*, Bombay, Indian national daily, (17 October 1929), quoted in M.K. Gandhi, pp. 71.

Varma, S.P. and Narain; 1968: *Fourth General Election In India*, New Delhi, Orient Publishers.

INDEX